The Vigil

Experiencing a life of divine design

By
Craig Smith

Acknowledgements

Many thanks to:

Dianna for more love and support than I deserve from such a great lady.

Paul Mills for production and creativity on the Vigil companion music CD. For many years of friendship between brothers, encouragement, and Kingdom adventures.

Leif Oines for editing, guidance, encouragement, and friendship.

My wonderful spiritual family in Arkansas that loves, challenges, and prays for my family and I while allowing me the freedom to pursue these adventures.

Contents

If you could ask God to show you the way to live your life to the fullest and He answered by giving you a model guaranteeing your success if you followed it, wouldn't you be excited to know what it is?

Preface

Perhaps not since the waning of the Great Awakening in mid-1700 has the church found herself in such shallow waters Biblically, in application, and genuine life experience. The evidence? Even with the abundance of the many and varied Christian media forms, genuine Christian influence upon culture is weak and in decline. Why? Maybe it is because we no longer look to God's design, at least with any intention of application.

It seems many of us have fallen prey to self-serving and self-gratifying behavior. Rather than relying on Scripture we draw from other sources which are incapable of producing necessary changes to cultivate the reform our culture requires for moral renewal, spiritual growth, and sustainability. Is it possible that in the church we are memorizing principles and precepts, writing and singing about them, but failing to intentionally and effectively use them in our daily lives?

I am not a fatalist, nor one given to pointless and undue criticism. I believe there is hope. The Bible repeatedly reveals God as the one changing the impossible into the possible. He is our hope, but then that is what he has always been, as the God of hope. Within his word is the map to navigate Christianity back into effectiveness, but it's a resource we must use, not just have knowledge of.

A good map contains information that with time, proper interpretation and consistent application ensures a successful arrival to a desired destination. During our time together I want us to focus, examine, and pursue an effective prayer that Jesus made available to all of us.

Vigil was chosen as the title of this project because it describes a period of time set aside for intense prayer and spiritual watchfulness. The word is derived from the Middle English *vigile,* which means, "devotional watching", and provides us with multi-layered imagery.

It proposes the setting aside of a daily time with God or even a special multiple day retreat for drawing away from life's normality in pursuit of a more focused and concentrated spiritual experience, individually or in a larger group.

As we begin this journey together my hope is that the Lord's Prayer will become your prayer just as it has become my prayer.

Introduction

Deep in the Buffalo River region of Arkansas is one of the most peaceful places I have ever visited. I have been there enough times now that it has become a familiar friend, a place for solitude and spiritual refueling. I hesitate to disclose the location for fear that it may become so popular it loses it's quiet reclusive character, but then that wouldn't be fair to others seeking shelter from the storm of life-clutter and distraction.

Within the small village of *Ponca,* sitting next to a very photogenic creek that runs through the distance of the township is a lodge called Cedar Crest. I usually stay there when visiting the area for several days. The main industries of Ponca are canoe and overnight cabin rentals and the Lost Valley General Store where you can pick up a few staples and an ice cream bar on a hot summer's day. If you're looking for a broad selection of food items, a longer drive will be necessary. All of this is comfortably nestled at the north end of Boxley Valley, a place worthy of some National Geographic attention, but then I am a little biased.

Almost daily elk can be seen quietly grazing in large open fields against the back drop of breathtaking limestone cliffs and forest covered hills that host and escort the Buffalo River on its meandering southern journey to the White River. Not far away from the Cedar Crest, beaver and trumpeter swan can often be seen traversing an old spring fed millpond, and occasionally I have spotted a bald eagle or two perched on one of the many trees at water's edge.

One cold January day while visiting there for a retreat, I was reading the Sermon on the Mount when I reached the Lord's Prayer. Each time I read this section, it is always with deep honor and devotion. While slowly perusing its words, I found myself amazed at the brilliance of the mind of Jesus and his passionate heart of love for his Father in heaven, the Father's will, and for those given to serving him. Within these brief sentences he strategically provided his new disciples and all who would later join them with his framework for a successful prayer life and the whole of life as well.

The prayer is as relevant today as it was the moment it flowed from his lips to the ears of those positioned around him. Though brief and woven with simplicity, it is embedded with power, divine brilliance, and instruction.

Unfortunately as with several things in Christianity, over the course of time, the lack of proper recognition and use has caused a veil of familiarity to conceal and lessen the true value of this treasure.

In some cases this masterful work has been reduced to a twenty-five second verbal recital of indifferent words. Not that it can't be sincerely spoken or recited with beauty and affect, but many times it is unfortunately delivered or presented with all the depth and sincerity as repeating ones name and street address when renewing a driver's license at the local DMV.

John Stott writes, *"It is comparatively easy to repeat the words of the Lord's Prayer like a parrot. To pray them with sincerity, however, it has revolutionary implications, for it expresses the priorities of a Christian. We are constantly under pressure to conform to the self-centeredness of secular culture. When that happens we are concerned about our own little name (liking to see it embossed on our notepaper or hitting the headlines of the press, and defending it when it is attacked), about our own little empire, (bossing, influencing, and manipulating people to boost our ego), and about our own silly little will (always wanting our own way and getting upset when it is frustrated). But in the Christian counter-culture our top priority concern is not our name, kingdom, and will, but God's.*[1]

Prayer was one of the primary objectives of Jesus when

teaching his disciples the principles for a fruitful victorious Christian life. He lived and modeled a life of prayer and he desires for all his followers to do the same because it is critical to our ongoing spiritual health, success, and the accomplishment of his mission.

This book is a reminder to all of us of the powerful tool available to guide us as we acknowledge in prayer, an eternal Father to be worshipped, the establishment of his will and causes, spiritual and physical resources for the task, and God's ability to navigate and protect us as we venture forward with him.

Even those who believe they are somewhat seasoned when it comes to prayer, are from time-to-time confronted with a situation where a path of prayer just can't seem to be quickly or comfortably located, when our minds won't readily assemble component and catalyst for fervent effective prayer to confront the moment at hand. In these times this offering from Jesus will escort us to the needed path and spiritual inertia.

I recently received a request from a friend of mine who leads a small ministry in Kampala, Uganda reaching out to children. He is trying to provide them with the hope of a future better than those of their parents. He is Ugandan and has an incredible story of survival during the era of Idi Amin, known as the "Butcher of Uganda" because of his ruthless and barbaric leadership over the country in the 1970's.

His request was simple "We have 18 children desiring to be part of our school which we want to help but do not have the extra resources. One of them a young girl, her name is Mayi, is 11 years old. Her father died and she helps feed her mother and 7 brothers and sisters by selling charcoal." And then he added, "She loves to sing."

Right after that I received a message from my own little village of Van Buren concerning an auto accident where a young driver lost control of his car and struck a culvert killing one of his passengers, his mother. Both situations left me wanting for words to begin to pray. I thought of the mental and emotional pain the young driver was experiencing and at the same time of a young girl named Mayi in Uganda who represented so many children in the world in need and wanting help.

The words defining my thoughts at that moment were, "Where do I begin?" Then I remembered the entry point to all good prayer whether here in my familiar geographical region or that of a young 11 year old half a world away. "You are our Father in heaven, you are holy. Your Kingdom come and your will be done because you alone know what to do and what is best. Please provide the needs in both of these overwhelming situations."

For those finding it difficult to establish a prayer time, a habit of praying, or a pattern of prayer, perhaps this work can act as an on ramp for cultivating a deeper prayer life. For those of us who may have gotten stale in our pursuit of prayer hopefully it will stimulate renewal. For those who have pursued ongoing prayer with deep seriousness, strength, and passion, perhaps this will become another resource as you seek the Father's heart.

Wherever you are on the spectrum, as believers we are all called to explore the depth and richness of God's kingdom and its transforming power as we pursue a vigilante prayer life.

The Directions

"The Lord's Prayer is a letter sent from earth to heaven."[2]

I am not alone in the story I am about to tell, it is one often experienced around the Christmas season, usually by fathers, and its message is about the wisdom in following directions.

Several times when my children were very young we would purchase them gifts that needed to be assembled. Typically I would wait until Christmas Eve and they were in bed before beginning the process of laying numerous toy parts on the floor, putting the box in view, and then begin what I always believed would be quick and easy steps, but usually were not.

Inevitably when I did not follow the directions packed in the box, I would always end up with spare parts and a present that would not quite work unless I disassembled it and started again, tired and frustrated. The older I have gotten I have discovered the wisdom and fruit of following the directions, or not buying anything that has to be built.

For those of us who embrace following Christ, one of the most challenging areas of our faith seems to be the establishment and maintenance of a growing, meaningful prayer life. We understand that it is vital to our spiritual health, growth, and the accomplishment of God's plans.

We acknowledge it is his design for our communication with him. We recognize the principle and privilege of mere humans to be granted access to the Creator of the heavens and earth through prayer. And, we identify prayer as the power source for the forward motion of his church.

Likewise, we see prayer presented in multifaceted forms and for varying purposes throughout the Scriptures. We know it can be a simple heart felt conversation on the one hand, and a deep mystical power encounter on the other. We understand the Bible instructs us to pray without ceasing, pray in the Spirit, fast and pray, watch and pray, pray in the evening, pray in the morning, and pray for the peace of Jerusalem.

It reveals that prayer can take place in temples, on the street, in kneeling positions, on the roof, in boats, on beaches, and on mountainsides. We see that throughout Scripture, God requires prayer if we intend to have a wholesome, vigorous, fulfilling relationship with him.

Having said that, why do you suppose so many of Jesus' followers find prayer challenging?

For some of us the answer could be as straightforward as it was for the first disciples of Jesus, maybe we need to ask him for help. When they did, he responded with an effective outline to follow, and this model will still guide any willing and sincere follower today.

The entire discourse in Matthew 6:9–13 reveals the availability of a roadmap of prayer that provides an easily followed pattern to acquire all things necessary for the accomplishment of his will during our earthly lives. And after all, isn't it his will that we should be seeking while we are on this earth?

Even the principle given in the books of Matthew to, ask, seek, and knock is ultimately for the purpose of his servants to fulfill his plans and desires. What else could it mean since we know all that exists is for his purposes? *"For by him all things were created: things in heaven and on earth, visible and invisible, whether thrones or powers or rulers or authorities; all things were created by him and for him."* Col. 1:16 (NIV)

Our problem is we have allowed the negative influences of the secular culture to seep into the church. We think we are to ask for things for us all the time instead of asking for what will help us fulfill God's will. He knows what we need, and he has said he will supply it when we focus on him and his mission.

We are not the central characters in Earth's theater, Jesus is! The pinnacle of fulfillment and source for our deepest joy is designed to be experienced as we serve, honor, and fulfill his will from a heart of love, gratitude, and expectation to see him glorified.

John Piper writes, *"Man is not the center of the universe, God is. And everything, as Paul says, is 'from Him and through Him and to Him.' Romans 11:36 (HCSB) 'To Him' means everything exists to call attention to Him and bring admiration to Him."*[3]

One of the primary things this prayer is to accomplish is to adjust our lives and desires, and rightfully place our focus on the one who deserves our complete attention, the God of all creation, the Father of life!

The method of prayer and location to pray come in numerous styles and even varied positions, but it is always about him.

I have enjoyed the practice and privilege of praying alone while walking along wooded paths, sharing a few simple grateful words and thoughts with God, thanking him for the marvel, variety, and beauty of his creation.

The Vigil

Other times it has been while isolated in a cabin or small cottage in some remote area in the cold of winter, or in the comfort of our home by the warm woodstove.

There have been times of deep intercession when I have prayed for mercy and guidance during a crisis or asking to grow in God's love and knowledge. Times when I have worshiped him for who he is and what he has done for me, prayers of gratefulness for his Word, as well as other prayers begging him to show me the way I should go while wondering how I so easily missed it.

Loud prayers, soft prayers, silent prayers, prayers while waiting, prayers in solitude, praying with thousands, written prayers and singing prayers in songs – all are valid. Prayer is multifaceted and worthy of exploring but of all that can be said about prayer perhaps the most important statement is to simply say, just do it!

The Lord's Prayer is a simple map, spoken from the mouth of our Savior and intended for all his disciples. Some authors have suggested Jesus gave it as a beginning point for his disciples, knowing that as they matured spiritually, so would their prayer lives and the need for an outline would one day no longer be a necessity. Others use it as a formality of ceremony

The Vigil

and do so sincerely.

While I agree it stands alone as a prayer of great strength, beauty, and covers the whole of prayer topically with no additional words needed, I think potentially it is like every other creation of God in that while it may appear simple and certainly accessible for easy entry by anyone seeking to converse with God, it also contains a depth and breadth far more than easily understood upon first glance.

We all realize this in our day-to-day lives when, or if, we think about it but we are often so busy that we miss the echoes of this truth. I see this play out just outside my house because if you stand in the field south of our home and look to the north, there are several wooded acres on the hill behind us. From the field you enjoy a view of a hillside of trees. Enter the woods themselves though and you discover a vast wonderland of varied hardwoods and cedars, meandering alongside vines, stones, and boulders of different colors, shapes, and sizes, not to mention the many and multiple scents wafting around you.

Be still and look upward long enough and suddenly movement can be detected in the limbs above as squirrels jump from limb to limb above you. Birds of all different types are represented like Downey woodpeckers, robins, cardinals, and a

The Vigil

dozen other types as well.

On the ground if you are patient and still, you might catch a glimpse of a tiny field mouse or white-tailed deer standing motionless hoping to avoid exposure. Almost totally concealed among some larger stones in the ravine, in the former home of a gray fox, there are sometimes opossum, raccoons, and even skunks, or at least the lingering evidence of their presence.

That's just the beginning, roll over enough rocks and fallen rotting logs and you'll eventually observe various assortments of snakes, both large and small, and if you really are on a zoological expedition, there are more insect varieties than you could easily count.

From a distance you see and appreciate the beauty of the wooded hillside, but once you enter the woods you begin to encounter countless details of life and beauty waiting to be explored, which can't be seen from far away.

God, his creation, and his Word are the same; this is just who he is and how he thinks and operates, simplicity coexisting with complex mystery. He is wonderful! Creator of all that exists, he holds it all together, and one word from him will signal the end of the world as we know it. However, he also desires intimate and personal relationship with humankind and provides a way for it to happen; mind blowing isn't it? Why would anyone *not* want to follow him?

The creator and maintainer of the world desires relationship with us and offers to lead us to and through the optimum life possible for each of us. All that is required is the surrendering of our agenda for his and then trusting in his flawless and effective directions.

Village2Village, the non-profit ministry I lead began as a desire to want to help people more than I was able to as the pastor of the church I am part of in Arkansas. The seed for V2V occurred while I was on a mission trip to a small village along a beautiful river in the bush area of Belize with a team from our church. Certainly not my first mission trip or the first time I was affected by poor and primitive conditions, but it was the place something shifted in me.

We were surveying a small village one morning about fifty minutes from the city of Belmopan, the country's capitol. I was walking around the village with a missionary friend who had over time developed friendships with the people through food assistance, visiting medical teams, and beginning a small church. The people were friendly, happy to see him and welcomed anyone he said was his friend.

The Vigil

At one point he took a couple of guys to show them some exterior painting to be done on a newly constructed church building and we walked toward the home of one of the villagers standing in the doorway of his tiny house.

He invited us in leading us through the area used to prepare food. There was one small table, dirt floor, and a few utensils hanging on the wall. Passing through I glanced down to the ground on the opposite side of the table and saw a few vegetable scraps, but also maggots and a few other insects. Two more steps inside the house and we saw young children playing on the floor.

This was not the situation we often see in pictures of third world countries with malnutrition or starving children, but it was the moment I experienced three thoughts; I live in extravagance, what more can I do and where do I start?

In that moment I realized that the directions Jesus gave for prayer apply in and for every situation. This was no different from praying over a meal and the model in Matthew chapter six contained the directions for this situation. Our Father in heaven has Kingdom plans and the resources to accomplish them in this small village; the solution is in the seeking and the asking for it based on the instructions from the Lord's Prayer.

I realize depth and detail need to be added for the specific strategy and practical steps, but the prayer principles for God's will in this village already exist within the content outline of the prayer.

~

Another word for directions is archetype - the word archetype is defined as the original pattern or model from which all things of the same kind are copied or on which they are based. The Lord's Prayer is our archetype, the original pattern, directions, or model for prayer. It leads us in a consistent and productive prayer life, covering the primary points for a healthy growing relationship with God, and it is also our map for places of deep intercession.

Like the myriad of things in the woods behind my home, this prayer delivered by Jesus, has multiple layers to be explored, exposed, and experienced.

Read the words of Sinclair Ferguson concerning this prayer. *"The Lord's Prayer serves two purposes. First, it provides a model prayer, an easily memorized outline that serves as a guide in how we are to approach God as Father and how we are to speak to Him. Second, it serves as an outline of the whole*

The Vigil

Christian life by providing certain 'fixed points' of concern for the family of God. It underlines life's priorities and helps us to get them into focus."[4]

And so, the beginning for our journey together has arrived; we move now from introductions to an invitation to discovery and then to application. A few verses earlier in the Sermon on the Mount just before giving his disciples this prayer, Jesus began with this remark, "When you pray..." These are key words for all who would call themselves Christian. He did not say, "If you pray", no need for theological speculation and debate here, Jesus obviously intended for every disciple to maintain a life of prayer.

As you begin to pray using this model, prepare to be encouraged, challenged, have your boundaries of understanding expanded, and grow in your appreciation of this divinely crafted masterpiece.

The Lord's Prayer provides entrance into a realm most only dream of because to actually attain it requires action on our part. Unfortunately many have succumbed to idle indifference, allowing the greatest adventure in the human experience to escape them, the invitation for interaction between the finite and the God of all creation. This prayer is not only worthy of our attention and pursuance, it is filled with eloquence and the pensive art of divine simplicity, while simultaneously plunging into unfathomable spiritual depths.

It is the ultimate experience waiting for those who will rise and step through its gateway, so let us pray together,

Our Father in heaven, Your name be honored as holy.
Your kingdom come.
Your will be done on earth as it is in heaven.
Give us today our daily bread.
And forgive us our debts, as we also have forgiven our debtors.
And do not bring us into temptation,
but deliver us from the evil one.
For Yours is the kingdom and the power and the glory forever.
Amen.[5]

Now let's journey together to discover more of the depth and beauty within this masterpiece to experience the life of divine design.

Our Father

There is an order to the spiritual life which when properly followed leads through the threshold of right relationship with God and produces unparalleled fulfillment in the human heart. This order begins in acknowledgement, honor, and worship of Him[6].

Life is filled with "first times"; one of mine took place on a sunny, spring day along an old concrete sidewalk on 46th Street on Louisville, Kentucky's west side. It was my tenth birthday and my parents had given me a new 24-inch Schwinn Flyer bicycle, and the event was its maiden voyage.

I mounted the bright red machine as my dad held it firmly and gave me last minute instructions before he began running alongside to help me gain some speed for better balance. He let go and I began the gradual downhill descent along the sidewalk for about a half block before reaching a cross street.

Picking up speed, a little unsure of myself, but also wondering if any of my neighborhood buddies were watching, with the wind in my face increasing with each push of the pedal, and the feel of a finely engineered machine beneath me, I could feel my confidence growing.

I looked down for a few seconds to watch the spin of shiny silver spokes and listened to the sound of the tires against the concrete walk. Then it happened.

I raised my eyes and straight ahead was a small mound of dirt about two feet tall at the highest point, separating the sidewalk from the cross street. I had seen it many times before, but never from this perspective.

If I had looked up a little sooner I might have made the turn, but not now. I hit the mound, flew off the bike and fell to the ground, while my new bike continued a few feet on its own before coming to rest in the middle of the street, and the front tire still spinning. No real damage was done to me or the bike, but it was definitely not the ideal dismounting technique.

The first thing I did after getting up from the ground was retrieve the bike from the pavement, but before checking for wounds, I looked up the street to see if my Dad had seen the mishap. Had there been a really bad spill, I'm sure he would have run the half block to my rescue. In this circumstance, he merely waited for me to return to the place he had stopped and let go of the bike to watch me continue on my own. Upon my return he offered a few additional riding tips like, "It's best to

The Vigil

not stare at the spokes too long while riding." or something to that effect.

Most of us have childhood memories of our fathers, varying from good to not so good. There are those who do not have memories of their father at all because they have never known them, but without exception, each of us has been affected in some way or another by our dad.

Except for my rebellious teen years, I have always loved and admired my dad. However my respect and appreciation for him increased substantially after committing my life to Jesus in the fall of 1972, because it was then I began to see my dad from a different perspective, a less selfish one.

During my defiant years, he represented the primary person attempting to prevent me from living the kind of life I thought would make me happy. After becoming a Christian I began to think differently and developed new goals and purposes for my life. With a changed heart, new values, and a desire to live for God, I saw my dad through a different lens. He was no longer the militant voice of reason and challenge regarding my choices and motives; instead he became a valuable friend, trusted ally, and source of wisdom and affirmation.

I finally realized that during the years when our relationship was so strained, my dad was being motivated by love and concern, and he was trying to prevent me from harm or ruining my life permanently.

A few months after my wife and I became Christians, I pursued Biblical studies at a college in Missouri. We were excited to embark on this new adventure and gave little thought of leaving our home in Louisville, nor did we think the move would signal the last time Louisville would be our permanent residence. Over three decades later it has become the destination for brief family visits during a holiday or vacation trip, the place we were raised, but no longer our home.

Over the years, one tradition that has developed occurs during departures from our visits to Kentucky. When we pull out of my parents driveway to begin our journey home, my mom waves and smiles from the front door or window facing the street, but my dad walks to the end of the driveway so he can observe us as we turn onto the main highway and get in one final wave. After his wave I follow up with a brief tap on the horn, marking the end to the departure ritual. Weather and health permitting; I believe that procedure will probably continue until he is physically unable to do so.

My dad and I understand that one of the principles of a

The Vigil

heart given to the Lord is to gratefully, willingly, and joyfully submit to his call regardless of the geographical location. We are humbled and honored to serve him but that doesn't change how much we wish we lived in closer proximity to each other for more frequent visits or morning coffee together in the kitchen. In fact, recently on a Saturday morning when I called home, the first thing he said was, "Hey son, I was just sitting at the kitchen table drinking a cup of coffee and wishing you were here having one with me." I can't tell you how much I wanted to jump in the car and point it eastward on Interstate-40 toward the northern border of the Bluegrass State, because I know how much those times together mean to both of us.

Mornings during my visits home typically unfold with me getting up and wandering down the hallway toward the kitchen where I find dad already seated at the table and reading the morning paper. We greet each other, but the words at this point remain pretty sparse, as I get myself one of several non-matching mugs hanging from small brass hooks displayed just above the countertop, souvenirs he has gathered from years of vacations. After filling it as close to the brim as I can, I carefully make my way to the oval table, take a seat, and before long one of us asks,

"Did you sleep okay?"

"Yep, how about you?"

"Oh, pretty good."

During the first few minutes, there is not a great deal of conversation between the two of us, just the good feeling of contentment from being across the table from each other. Eventually one of us usually kicks off a conversation and we find ourselves remaining in the kitchen for quite a while talking about everything from minor household chores and repairs, to the complexities of current world affairs.

My favorite conversations are when he begins reminiscing about his childhood or time in the South Pacific during WW II, the beginning of the Korean conflict, or his job as a young boy in Mr. Jarboe's grocery store on 38th and Market Street. Sometimes I get to hear how he met my mother or the many stories of neighborhood adventures with my uncle and their friends.

Like the time he was sent up the street by his mother to get his brother and step-brother for dinner. My dad discovered them involved in an intense game of marbles with some other young boys in the neighborhood and got lured into the game himself. Shortly, the oldest brother was sent to fetch the missing members of the clan for a dinner that was starting to cool.

Almost twenty years old at the time, he got in the game, and all was going well until my dad looked over his shoulder and saw one steaming four feet eleven inch tall, "Mad little Dutch lady stomping feverishly toward them and yelling, 'You boys better get home before I...'". Some of my dad's stories are so detailed and funny, I feel like I am watching an episode from one of the old, 1930"s "Little Rascal's" films.

His stories are wonderful and numerous. Some I have heard many times but I always enjoy hearing them again. Sometimes there are added details to color and enhance them. Then out of nowhere will come a new tale or adventure from his past I have never heard before. Two to three hours can pass before we take a break and shift from the kitchen to another location in the house or onto the back porch if the weather is warm enough.

I tell you about my relationship with my biological father, because there is a certain indescribable peace and security enjoyed when right relationship exists between a father and son, but it is disappearing from our cultural landscape because of the rapid diminishing of the family.

One of the primary aims of satan the past several decades

has been to systematically reduce and destroy the appropriate role God intended for fatherhood. Why? As that role becomes confused, skewed, and weakened, it increases the damage to humanity on several fronts.

Without the presence of earthly fathers functioning in their proper God designed roles, the enemy causes distortions in how we see, understand, and relate to our Father in heaven. Earthly fathers were created to provide a reflection of his fatherly characteristics toward his children. Fathers are to be a mirror image of his love, provision, security, faithfulness and presence.

Distort and devalue the earthly role of fatherhood, and it can harm how we view the role and characteristics of our heavenly Father. When earthly fathers are self-centered, unfaithful, uncaring, and absent, it introduces suspicion, doubt, and insecurity into the children. Those negative characteristics then spill over into our perception of God the Father, causing suspicion about His faithfulness and questioning His genuine concern for us.

Satan's motive in undermining proper earthly fatherhood has been to cause humanity to deny trust in God as our heavenly Father, and a heart without trust in God is a heart with a vacuum of hope. And, *"Hope deferred makes the heart sick."*[7]

Recently I was thinking about two men I know. They both have tremendous potential to make a difference with their lives and affect positively the people around them. Both are in their thirties and I have spent quite a bit of time listening to and asking questions about their childhood, relationship with their fathers growing up, and what kind of impact they thought it had on them as adult men. Both are skilled at their craft, mentally sharp, and gifted with several abilities. Both have children and want their lives to mean something, reflect value, worth, and be happy.

Both have also had a lot of difficulty in their lives with addictions, commitment, stability, and anger. They both are following in the footsteps of their fathers. Ironically one lives in the heart of the United States while the other lives in a jungle in Central America.

All of our hearts, regardless of geography, have been fashioned by God and wired for the same essential needs. One of these important needs is the role of fatherhood as God intended. Without it we are exposed to the emotional elements that deteriorate the desired tenderness and wholeness of heart God wants us to experience.

Our heavenly Father loves and deeply cares about the lives

of people. He is perfect in every way, and thus a perfect Father. He never wanted humanity to suffer the darkness of the evil one. God's plan has always been for humanity's good and for our lives to be enriched by life in his Kingdom. Satan's design for humanity on the other hand has always been to harm.

Our Father in heaven though provided escape from the enemy's plan, and extended a way for us to find freedom, reconciliation, continued communion, protective covering, and eternal fatherhood, through belief in the redemptive work of Jesus Christ.

When Jesus introduced the words "Our Father in heaven" at the beginning of his lesson on prayer for his disciples in Matthew 6:9, he introduced a new dimension of God's character and personality for all who would believe in him.

"It was Jesus who taught men the reality and nature of the Fatherhood of God, and made it the foundation and essence of religious life. This is the very first time that the words are addressed to God in prayer, so far as the Bible is concerned."[8]

With the words *Our Father in heaven,* Jesus confirmed and illuminated these truths:

- There is only one who is Creator of all things.

- He is the Father of all life.

- He requires worship.

- He desires sincere warm loving relationship and personal interaction with humanity.

- He requires respect and honor in this relationship.

- He clearly wants to protect, provide, and guide those under his care.

- Those who embrace him will never be fatherless, and will enter into the most loving, privileged, deeply committed, functional family in existence.

Those first four words of Jesus in this prayer reveal the possibility of deep, genuine, intimate, and multi-dimensional relationship. It is an incomprehensible offering, far too wonderful to be true it seems, but it is. His gracious, loving offer remains intact forever upon acceptance, and he will never abandon those who have placed themselves under his protection, nor will he change the rules along the way or fall out of love with those who are his.

- Four words produce security and satisfy the heart.

- Four words provide the definition for real trust.

- Four words provide us with the availability of an

authentic holistic family unit; the family of God, "a chosen people."[9]

- Four words expose the One who is the designer and initiator of all life and His heart intent toward humanity.
- Four words remind us that "Father", from the Greek word *Pater* means the one who nourishes, protects, and supports.

The current deficiency of those filling a truly godly role of fatherhood has ushered in one of the worst tragedies in modern times; unleashing instability, insecurity, emotional imbalance, and a problematic entanglement to which only God can restore. God is the father our heart deeply yearns for. He is the only one who can inject wholeness and stability into fragmented, imbalanced, and, nonsensical lives. He is the only one who can bring hope to our anemic family situations. His love and care can usher in the life-breath for which we so desperately and urgently gasp.

I attended a function once where a table was decorated with a centerpiece containing a large clear glass container filled with water, long stemmed flowers, and several goldfish. The display was attractive and interesting to look at, but after a while the fish began to gather at the water's surface for air because of the decline of oxygen in the water. Without attention the fish would have eventually suffocated.

Humanity has one spiritual oxygen source, and that is God the Father. Without his oversight, left to fend for ourselves, we are deprived of the necessary life-breath for which we were designed. His fatherly influences bring unprejudiced justice, firm honesty, unshakable security, and unmatchable love. He is without fear and in him is the power source to stave-off any level of attack from those things lurking in the shadows attempting to tamper with our minds to generate fear and insecurity in us.

With God as our Father we remain in an impenetrable field of refuge and sanctuary in accordance to his will for our lives. His role as our father, in the life of humanity, defines his intention toward humanity, which has always and will forever continue to be pure, honorable, and advantageous for those who place themselves under his care.

Where earthly failures have caused doubt and cynicism, there is life and hope waiting in the faithfulness of the Heavenly Father. Displacement and the feeling of being orphaned need not continue unless one foolishly chooses and decides to remain in that condition. Where this condition exists, the Father in heaven can and will alter the flawed paled image and transition it to one of triumph for the human soul as the redemptive work of Jesus is applied to the repentant heart. When our intent is to allow his influence to rule our lives, we can rest in his unfailing love, unrivaled qualities, pure intentions, and unlimited abilities.

One of my favorite quotes attempting to define God's character and qualities comes from writer Adam Clarke who writes that our Father is:

"the eternal, independent, and self-existing Being: the Being whose purposes and actions spring from himself, without foreign motive or influence; he who is absolute in dominion; the most simple, the spiritual of all essences; infinitely perfect; and eternally self-sufficient, needing nothing that he has made; illimitable in his immensity, inconceivable in his mode of existence, and indescribable in his essence; known fully only by himself, because an infinite mind can only be fully comprehended by itself. In a word, a Being who, from his infinite wisdom, cannot err or be deceived, and from his infinite goodness, can do nothing but what is eternally just, and right, and kind."[10]

So, as with all things pertaining to God we discover

ourselves facing the wonder of complexity and simultaneously the essence of simplicity. They emanate from a singular source, inseparable, and mysterious, but delivering comfort and peace when we belong to him. We know that only God our father is just and good, the mystery and expanse of his vastness should deliver great comfort to our hearts. This huge God who is love's essence, who eludes adequate human definition, is our Father.

When we see and feel around us seemingly insurmountable inconsistencies, unfolding disappointments and gross injustices growing in the world, and recognize the huge lack of mental and material resources needed from men and nations to construct bridges to remedy these complex situations, let us not be robbed of peace! A resting place exists, a safe harbor from the storm, within the storm. True sanctuary waits in the care, in the presence, and in trusting our Father in heaven.

"In calling Him 'Father,' we express a relationship we have all known and felt surrounding us even from our infancy; but, in calling Him our Father 'who art in heaven' we contrast Him with the fathers we all have here below, and so raise our souls to that 'heaven' where He dwells, and that Majesty and Glory which are there as in their proper home. The first words of the Lord's Prayer-this Invocation with which it opens-what a brightness

and warmth does it throw over the whole prayer, and into what
a serene region does it introduce the praying believer, the child
of God, as he thus approaches Him!"[11]

This prayer given by Jesus to assist his disciples is a masterpiece of divine brilliance. For it is both the outline for an on-ramp for the novice or beginning prayer student, while simultaneously providing a path for the most seasoned prayer veteran entering into an intense place of prayer.

It is a spiritual road map for a successful prayer time, be it three minutes, three hours, or three days.

Our entry point in prayer is to, recognize, honor, and worship the Father we have in heaven. He alone is worthy of and deserving of our admiration and undivided attention before we venture into any other area of proclamation or petition, regardless of importance. He is to be worshiped first, which is why Jesus set the precedent in this prayer. He introduced God and humankind interactive in the highest order of relationship; a divine mystery, but also a divine blessing, for God is:

Our Father in heaven

Hallowed be Your Name

"In praying that God's name be hallowed we ask that He will so act that His creatures may be moved to render that adoration which is due His name."[12]

Rain falls on a cool mid-October morning. Sunrise is approaching, but it still remains in the distance for now. On a tall pole not far from a modest one and a half story country house is a lone dim night lamp, its rays reflecting off the water covered foliage just a few feet outside the backdoor of the house. A mild breeze generates slight motion as it moves through the trees and shrubbery causing a glistening effect, nothing dramatic just a pleasing visual nuance for dawn's breaking.

With the exception of the raindrops hitting the leaves and tin gutters along the edge of the house, the only sounds to be heard are a few crickets providing a sort of natural droning mantra to beckon the coming sunlight. Some Bible passages that provide definition to the moment are,

"Everything on earth will worship you they will sing your praises"[13]

"the Lord is in his holy temple; let all the earth be silent before Him."[14]

"Be still, and know that I am God."[15]

"Not to us, O Lord, not to us, but to your name be the glory, because of your love and faithfulness."[16]

"...we wait for you; your name and renown are the desire of our hearts. My soul yearns for you in the night; in the morning my spirit longs for you."[17]

In the stillness of this morning there is only one name to be sought and on which to dwell, the name of the Lord, *"O Lord, our Lord, How excellent is Your name in all the earth!"* [18]

To those who do not have a relationship with Christ, I suppose his name may not mean so much, but to those that do; his name represents life at its experiential zenith. His name can bring soberness and calm to situations of chaos and confusion. His name can transform the festering decay of despair and disappointment; introduce inspiration, the promise of a better future, and a unique hope which moves beyond fields of speculation into the arena of certainty. His name can alter the outcome of the most dismal of situations because his name has no boundary or limitation.

The Vigil

Names are typically given to persons, places, and things to identify, describe their character, or even to place value on them. If it is a place, the name might reflect a natural wonder or beauty such as the Grand Canyon or expose possible peril like Death Valley that gained its name in the mid 1800's when gold hunters mistook it for a shortcut that often led to misfortune.

Names also become markings of endurance describing and reflecting the investments of human struggle, and painful sacrifice like the Battle of Gettysburg and D-Day. Others define possibility like the Cape of Good Hope in South Africa, the rocky outcropping that marks the turning point for ships traveling between the South Atlantic and Indian Oceans.

Almost everything has a name, from viruses, bacteria, plants, animals, nations, cities, villages, and everything within them. Some names are deemed so important; they are patented, like toy companies, beverage and food companies, automobile makers, electronics manufacturers, and computer designers. The list almost seems infinite because everything has a name for some type of identification or clarification!

I live in a region where the Arkansas River flows between two towns. On the south side lies the city of Fort Smith with a population of about 81,000 and on the north side is much smaller town, Van Buren, with about 16,000 folks. We have lived in both communities at one time or another, but Van Buren with its old town main street, complete with a one hundred year old county court house at the bottom of the hill on Main, and the small Frisco Victorian style train station at the top of the hill on the other end, is where we have lived for over 28 years.

One of the town's mainstays, also on Main Street, is a small restaurant named the Cottage Café. For years it has been the place you could eat a big breakfast for two or three bucks, hear a funny story or two (usually true but maybe a little exaggerated) and catch up on most of the town's news and world views without a newspaper, cell phone, or laptop. And no, they still don't have WiFi so if you want to research something online you have to jot it down on a napkin and check the web later.

The locals can still tell you about the morning the sheriff was sitting at the first table just inside the entrance, quietly drinking coffee and eating a hearty breakfast when suddenly a deer appeared at the front door entrance and stepped inside. It stopped opposite the officer's table, they stared at each other a second, with neither knowing what to do, then the deer bolted through the room, knocking things over before jumping through the big plate glass window, and disappearing behind the train station never to be seen again.

The Cottage Café is replicated in one form or another in thousands of small cafés strewn throughout America. There are always similarities, but I find this one to be my favorite. Why? Because it's in the small town that I live in. People's names often find their way into the conversation in this little cafe.

Sometimes they're the names of the local high school coach that pulled off the big Friday night win against a team that was supposed to beat them by three touchdowns. In these cases the names are used with pride, congratulatory smiles, and nods of approval from those sitting around the tables within earshot of the conversation.

Other times though a name is brought up that will bring a subtle sneer or facial expression of scorn and disgust. Those are often associated with politicians, perceived injustice, or some unfair business transaction.

There are names from history like Hitler and Stalin that bring thoughts of heartbreak and sadness because of their cruelty, inhumanity, and tyranny forced upon the world. Often the memories from these names are accompanied by the deep concern of history repeating itself unless sufficient reminders and preventative measures are in place to assure the hate and death exemplified by these names are not allowed to manifest by new names of equally demented motive and heartlessness.

Other names in history however bring feelings of gratefulness, inspiration, and applause. They cause us to be amazed at their commitment, selflessness, and quantity of compassion. Their seemingly tireless efforts to bring hope to the plight of the world's poor, diseased, persecuted, and displaced. Names like Mother Theresa, Hudson Taylor, and Mary Slessor, the young Scottish woman who in the 1800's at age 29 entered Africa as a missionary, poured her life out for others, remained there faithfully for almost 40 years, and who was so loved and respected she became known among the people she gave her life for as, "The White Ma of Africa."

Of all names both old and new though, there is one that rises and stands infinitely higher than any other for a commitment to justice, care, faithfulness, and compassion. It is a name worthy of the highest and noblest honor. In fact no other name has or will ever equal it, nor will it fade or be forgotten with the passing of time. It describes and represents impeccable character and boundless dominion. It is to be

The Vigil

glorified, worshiped, and declared among the nations. This name embodies the promise of genuine hope, joy, and the anticipation of great and unexplainable eternal things yet to come.

Though this name is worshiped and revered by many, amazingly there are others who foolishly abhor it. For them this name causes disdain, disgust, discomfort, and even hatred. They rebel against this name and all it represents, but when this earth has seen its final light of day and heard the concluding words of the last chapter, there will be only one name that will stand.

The name to which I'm referring is *God*, but then there are several misrepresentations and misappropriations when some choose to use this three-letter word to refer to their idol of choice, so let me clarify. The one Christianity embraces has created all things and forever retains dominion over what he made, is the only eternal God, and is also known as, Yahweh, Jehovah, Elohim, Adhonay, Almighty, and The Holy One to mention a few.

Additional names reveal his unchanging attributes, pristine character, and innumerable qualities. He is also called Wonderful, Mighty Counselor, and the Prince of Peace. He is referred to as Rock to represent his faithfulness and the absoluteness of his protection and refuge from all that would do harm to those he loves. He is called the King for his supremacy and dominion over all things, and Righteous for his flawless character, purity, and holiness.

He is called Shield and Deliverer for he is an unfailing guardian and liberator. He is called the Ancient of Days because he superseded all life; in fact he brought life into existence and he is the essence of it, without him there would simply be no life. Mysteriously, his life had no beginning and for that matter will have no ending, which is shown in another of his names, Alpha and Omega.

For those within humanity who realized their separateness from him, their hopelessness to remedy their situation, and their desperate and insatiable hunger for reconciliation, come his names that bring the fragrances of life and sweetness to the soul. They are the names Savior, Messiah, Redeemer, and the one of unequivocal beauty and stature, the name of Jesus.

My friend Nsimbi who oversees a ministry with a church and school for orphaned children and the very poor in Kampala Uganda knows Jesus Christ in his native tongue of Luganda, the language of the Baganda Tribe to which he belongs, as *Yesu*

Kiristo. Though I can't even say it properly in his language, we both are recipients of the magnificent grace and power, which comes from the name and grace work of Jesus Christ.

Most of us have been in situations or conversations when someone has attempted to bolster their value, or shore up their self-worth by dropping the name of a dignitary or some well-known personality, maybe you have even been guilty of this yourself, unfortunately I have. Those names may bring some temporary recognition or acclaim, but eventually the benefit wears thin and the name becomes distant or forgotten.

The name of the Lord however carries authority, purpose and the power to fulfill that purpose for eternity. The name, its value, and all that is promised and represented within it will never diminish. In other words, association with this name has eternal benefits. Embracing and honoring his name really does make a difference, it brings change, attention, influence, and purpose.

There was a man named Moses who learned the value and influence of God's name. Moses received some instructions from God concerning how to deal with a foreign leader who had enslaved an entire nation of people. God told Moses he was going to use him as his mouthpiece to present an ultimatum to

Pharaoh that would eventually free the people. Moses listened, but after hearing the plan concern and intimidation filled his heart on two fronts.

Why would Pharaoh listen?

Why would those in captivity listen to him?

This was Moses' response to God, "Suppose I go to the Israelites and say to them, 'The God of your fathers has sent me to you,' and they ask me, 'What is his name?' Then what shall I tell them?" God said to Moses, "I AM WHO I AM. This is what you are to say to the Israelites: 'I AM has sent me to you.'"[19]

Moses knew God's people would recognize the name, "I AM," but what about Pharaoh, the country's leader, that the Israelite's were enslaved to? Would the name, "I AM" mean anything to him?

Moses was probably thinking several things that led to this question. God's name may mean a lot to God's people, after all they had walked with God a long time, they knew of his history and his dealings between God and them, but would God's name mean much to those who do not acknowledge or serve him?

Perhaps Moses was thinking, "What will prevent Pharaoh from just having me instantly executed for insolence before the king?" After all, Egypt had no shortage of deities that they believed in, even Pharaoh was listed among them, so why should he think Pharaoh would listen and comply with God's demand and relinquish control over the Israelites?

When God responded to Moses' question, God knew the name, "I AM" was not among the Egyptian list of deities, he was not unaware of the smallest detail, but regardless of Pharaoh's possible response to Moses, Moses was expected to deliver the message, because Moses knew the history, power, and authority behind the name of God.

He was wise to respond to God's request with great reverence and obedience, and as the story continued to unfold so did the accompanying evidence that came along with representing the name and request of God.

Moses was able to walk into Pharaoh's chamber knowing it was God's ability and God's authority that would complete the task. His name made a difference; it brought change, influence, and purpose. His name brought deliverance to the Israelites from the slavery of Egypt, because his name was accompanied with power and authority.

God's name also brought healing to a man crippled from birth as he was sitting and begging for money at a temple gate. He asked Peter, one of God's servants for help hoping to receive a coin or two, but instead Peter told him he had no silver or gold, but what he did have he would give him. Then Peter spoke to the man and told him in the name of Jesus Christ of Nazareth stand up and walk. Peter grabbed the man's hand and helped him to his feet and the beggar suddenly realized he was no longer a cripple and began not only walking, but jumping up and down and praising God for His mercy and the miracle of being able to walk.

Power and authority in the name of God isn't just applicable in the past. This recent story was shared by John, one of the missionaries helped by Village2Village in Belize, whose name I've changed at his request. He and his family are very excited about all of the opportunities that have been opening to them since their move from their home in a small town in Northwest Arkansas to Banana Bank, Belize where they now headquarter.

John and Eugeno, his Kekchi Indian assistant, had embarked one morning on a day trip to another village. Though they had cell phones, communication is not always the most reliable. Long after their journey began they received a call and were told Eugeno's mother had fallen hitting her head on a stone. They turned their truck around and began heading the opposite direction.

The Vigil

Once they finally arrived in the village where she lived, they placed her in the bed of the pickup truck and began the long journey to a medical facility. Upon their arrival, an emergency medical person jumped into the bed of the truck and attempted to revive her. Unfortunately his best efforts were not helping her. After a period of time Eugeno looked at the man he calls Pastor John, and said, "It's okay boss, it is her time."

John said he had no idea what took over that day, but suddenly flowing from his mouth were these words, "It's not okay today!" He began to pray for a miracle in the name of Jesus Christ and the woman who was non-responsive to any of the prior treatment of the medical personnel suddenly sat up in the truck and opened her eyes. The medical worker was so startled he lunged away from Eugenio's mother to the other side of the bed of the pickup.

Was this freak chance, a trick of some kind, or was it the result of appealing to the one whose name is above all names? I for one am always ready to give honor where honor is due and in heaven maybe God will straighten out all our theological preferences, obstacles, and nuances but in the meantime I believe that God's name still has the power to change the things that the wisdom and resource of mankind cannot.

The Vigil

From the beginning to the end of time, for all who have trusted in the name of Jesus to receive his gift of grace, we are promised that the power of his name has washed the darkness from our putrid hearts and justified us before God our Father. Forgiveness is a humbling and yet powerfully freeing agent and it comes only from believing in and embracing the name of Jesus Christ.

So wonderful is this name that we are instructed in all we do or say, to do it rightly representing the name of Jesus, [20]and in that same name, to thank God for everything.[21] That is a hefty order, but since it originates from the same loving, heavenly Father we talked about in the previous chapter, we can be assured it is for our benefit in the long run.

Praise the Lord!
Yes, give praise, O servants of the Lord.
Praise the name of the Lord!
Blessed be the name of the Lord now and forever.[22]

Hallowed be Your name

Your Kingdom Come

"We live now between the inauguration of the kingdom and the consummation of the kingdom. We therefore pray that the kingdom which has already been established will express its presence more and more throughout the earth, until the day comes when, 'the kingdom of the world has become the kingdom of our Lord and of His Christ, and He will reign forever and ever. (Rev. 11:15)."[23]

"Your Kingdom Come." The combination of these words today can birth images of a compelling novel or epic movie in which some lowly village peasant working dawn to dusk in a smelting shop for a cruel embittered taskmaster, is somehow chosen because of his quiet and humble character to liberate his fellow villagers from the tyranny of an evil and unmerciful ruler named...*Melondorf!*

He lives high atop a creepy looking mountain veneered with dangerous jagged cliffs and only one rocky narrow trail leading to a drawbridge and a gate the size of a five story building, which is the only entry into a massively tall, dark, stone tower, the top of which hosts the living quarters for this feared oppressor whose mere voice causes trembling and terror throughout the land.

Armed only with the passion of a vision, a torn and tattered map of antiquity, and an old walking stick with some undisclosed powers, the peasant sojourns across treacherous and hostile landscapes to obtain an audience with a good and noble king in a distant land to tell him of his quest to liberate his fellow villagers and to seek his help and blessing.

The king who has awaited such a liberator for the oppressed villager's for year's grants his request because he had once read a story mentioned in some relic of a book kept in a special room deep within the castle's ancient library which spoke of such a one which would someday come to the rescue of those oppressed by the evil of Melondorf.

After numerous battles, creature encounters, and perilous escapes, the village peasant's journey finally leads him to the dark castle of Melondorf, the final destruction of evil and the liberation of his village from totalitarian rule. Oh, and somewhere within the saga he wins the hand of the good king's beautiful daughter...*Anastella*, and a large cave filled with treasure. The end!

~

To those with more tranquil imaginations, kings and kingdoms invoke mental images of medieval castles in faraway places with beauty, rich history, and the romantic stories to accompany them, such as the castles of England, Scotland, Ireland, France, and Germany.

Obviously king's and kingdoms are no longer part of our normal vernacular, but in the days when Christ spoke these words, Your Kingdom Come, they represented someone with the positional authority within a place or region.

In the opening lines of this prayer Jesus has presented the nature and character of this King. He is not some demanding unreasonable monarch disconnected from his people, he is quite the opposite. He is described to us by Jesus as the loving and unquestionable Father of life, who desires to be known among his subjects as one whom affectionately cares and provides for them with fatherly characteristics.

Because he is the flawless Father, the Creator of all things, the pinnacle source for trust and security, nothing or no one even begins to approach or compare with his stature and prominence. Nor is there anything within his realm that is thrown aside, ignored, or goes unnoticed. In fact, in his mind everyone is equally important because he designed and equipped them each for a specific purpose. He nurtures them and weaves them together to produce a divinely interlaced tapestry of strength, beauty, and usefulness.

There is a small Kekchi Indian village in the jungles of Belize called San Pablo that ranks among one of my favorite places to have visited in my life to date. It is located by a pristine river that winds its way through tall thick tree and bush-covered hillsides to the valley below.

On my second visit, about a dozen red macaws flew from one jungle covered hilltop to the next, their call momentarily interrupting the valley's tranquility. The small village probably contains a couple dozen families in all. They are hardworking people, but they live a pretty simple lifestyle, and appear quite happy and content most of time.

One of its residents is a kindly man by the name of Quahkin. He and his family live in a small hut consisting of walls constructed from wood poles about two inches in diameter cut from the jungle surrounding the village, placed side by side, and then carefully tied together for maximum strength. A thatched roof of palm tree leaves, and a floor of tightly packed soil finish out the home.

His wife, Naomi cooks in a corner of the hut over three large stones that have been strategically placed to hold a handmade wire grill to cook with. Cloth hammocks hang on the walls and serve as beds for sleeping at night or the occasional afternoon nap.

The hut contains little else beyond a few personal clothing items, some handmade tools, which includes several machetes used for cutting firewood, dealing with unwanted animals and perhaps to discourage the occasional suspicious and uninvited visitor. Quahkin's home is probably the nicest in the village and he is the village's appointed leader or overseer.

I was introduced to this wonderfully beautiful and remote place by a friend who wanted me to see and meet these people and experience their simple culture. After meeting Quahkin, he was gracious enough to show me around his village, which was literally cut out of the jungle in 1995. He knew everyone and could account for everything that went on within his realm of authority. They are a close community helping each other and carefully watching out for one another. In fact, had I not been introduced to Quahkin by our mutual friend, it is doubtful I could have just walked into their region without being sternly confronted, and without good explanation as to why I was there, be escorted out of the village.

One day Quahkin led us through the jungle along a narrow path to the river's edge. Once there he continued along a trail beside the river pointing out the best fishing areas, the popular washing and bathing sites, and even the spots where someone had died in the river's swift current. Then he held his arm up pointing through a clearing in the trees to a place in the middle of the river where a couple of big boulders stood causing the rapid rushing of water.

He continued down the path to a location where we could walk and jump from rock to rock until we arrived at the spot he had shown us through the trees. It was his favorite location in the lush green jungle valley, and it was there Quahkin and I along with two other villagers clicked a photo or two to commemorate my visit. This was Quahkin's realm of authority and the expressions on his face displayed his pride in knowing and caring for it, as well as sharing it to those of his choosing.

One other thing worth noting about my Central American experience is that because I was with Quahkin in his village, I was granted privileges and extended invitations I wouldn't have had otherwise, including the honor and invitation to dine in his home as his guest. I returned to the village just a few days after my initial visit and was greeted by warm friendly waves, smiles, and the joy of several young giggling children. Because I was well known among them? No, because I was known by the village elder Quahkin.

Just as there are things I get to participate in the village, as a friend of Quahkin, there are principles, privileges, and characteristics in the Kingdom of God I am subject to as well as invited to enjoy, not because I am worthy of them, only because I am known by the head of the global village.

When Jesus said in this prayer, "Your Kingdom Come", it was to ignite in his disciples, and in all who would later follow Jesus, with a passion to yearn for a relationship with the king of the kingdom to which he prayed would come. To allow him by his Spirit to saturate every fiber of our being and to sincerely long for the things He longs for. To pray for his personality, character qualities, and purpose to infuse and influence every earthly institution, civilization, and each individual dwelling within them.

When we sincerely pray, "Your kingdom come", we are acknowledging and asking God to permeate all things, to submit to his authority, and to have our sole purpose to bring glory and honor to him.

God certainly does not need our invitation or permission to

rule over us. He doesn't need us to ask for his preeminence over our lives, our careers, our possessions, the leaders of our towns, cities, and nation, or the nations of the world. He could enforce His desires upon each of us and all things without any ability on our part to resist, refuse, or object in spite of any or all our perceived strengths, superiority or combined resources. The tower of Babel was the first story of humanity's attempt and failure to resist external rule or influence over it by the divine king, and even though voices continue clattering its plausibility, it will never happen.

Though a mystery to most, God decided to offer his redeemed the opportunity to invoke his dominance in and over all things. He desires for us to be involved in the process of seeing his divine influence operating in all realms of created existence.

While writing one day, I transitioned from a small desk in our sunroom, out to our front porch. It was a fall day and even though a bit cool, the afternoon sun's brilliance on our little valley was too tempting for me to stay inside any longer. I poured a mug of fresh coffee, grabbed a granola bar, situated myself in a rocker, and got ready to be inspired. Then it happened.

I looked up and out across the field floating from one end of the valley to the other, like tiny hang-gliders, came dozens of what appeared to be cylinder-like grass stems about ten inches long with feather-like stems extended around them catching the wind and carrying them high above the ground.

Instantly I began to imagine and wonder what it would be like to float so effortlessly through the valley like that. It almost seemed like a dream; surreal, but it definitely put my mind in neutral, and engaged my imagination.

Let me attempt the same here for a moment, to engage your imagination, though it would help if you were sitting on my porch.

Picture yourself sitting in the waiting room of your dentist; you pick up a magazine, and begin flipping through the pages. On page forty-six, just opposite the page advertising the latest electronic gadget is the name of a huge new self-contained community development on some previously undiscovered island.

The geographical location lends itself to the daily possibility of seamless sunrises, perfectly temperate afternoons, breathtaking sunsets, and peaceful evenings. You can live in the safe, secure environment of your choice, so perfect you'll never need a vacation getaway.

Amazingly, you discover after moving there that not only will you no longer be in debt, but neither is the sovereign island. You realize you need little to be content, and even though some of your neighbors may have more stuff than you it just doesn't matter. You have friends and neighbors that are always looking out for your welfare and you have nothing to hide from them because they are completely trustworthy.

They celebrate each other's accomplishments and work together to help the other guy win. In fact, every time you get together you experience some realm of encouragement. You and your fellow islanders even work together to help those who have sudden health problems or job loss.

As you comb over the island newspaper on Saturday mornings at the corner café, there are no stories about a rash of burglaries and robberies over the weekend and no out of control divorce statistics. Absent are headlines about alcoholism, drug problems at the local high school, a pedophile who just moved into your neighborhood, gangs taking over parts of the island, a terrorist cell discovered at the local college campus, a drug cartel threatening to invade, or the abduction of a child.

When election year rolls around no one challenges the current leadership because the cultural atmosphere and soundness sociologically is attributed solely to his flawless governing ability. No one runs against him because they like him so much no one wants to. There is no hidden agenda or questionable character. He is strong, resolute, fair, just, and his decisions are always so accurate no one questions his capacity to lead.

Okay, back to reality! First of all this place does not exist this side of heaven. Second, only those with hearts and minds given to learning and living the characteristics of Christ would want to move there, but if there were such a place there would certainly be many attempting relocation within the safety of its borders as soon as possible. We would be persistent in wanting and asking for that place or that type of place to be our habitat.

God has a desire, and this is it, that all His original intentions for mankind would be restored. Heaven is perfect in every way and we are to pray for his Kingdom to come on earth as it is in heaven. Knowing there is a perfect place led by a perfect God who is Father, Son the Redeemer, and Holy Spirit the comforter, who has a perfect plan for everything, should be catalyst enough for us to pray to see it established on earth even if we don't fully understand everything contained in the phrase, Your Kingdom Come.

Consider for a moment the option of attempting to continue to correct and better the current worldly issues on our own. True we have accomplished a lot medically and technologically. We have developed complex economical systems to guard against falter and collapse. We continue to explore and deeply probe the human brain and psyche for better understanding. Elaborate governmental structures have been assembled to defuse foreign aggressors and internal division. No problems here, thanks to the exploits of human resourcefulness. We are nearly a perfect global village aren't we?

Actually we are in horrible shape and the reason is wealth, power, and prestige absent of the pursuit of godliness can't produce healthy social and moral sustainability. In other words, without God it is always a downward spiral.

I am not saying our prayers for God's Kingdom to come will usher the earth to an immediate state of perfection. I am saying we are instructed by Christ to pray that the Kingdom of God and all it represents and means would fill our lives and the earth that God's flawless *will* would come to pass on earth as it is in heaven. The time frame and results we leave to God.

The Vigil

One writer said three things should always be remembered when thinking about the kingdom of God,

- The kingdom is a spiritual reality that is already present among men.

- The coming of this kingdom to the individual is not an end in itself. Indeed only the beginning. After we are in the kingdom individually, we must turn outward with the message.

- The kingdom is also a future event.[24]

Jesus cherished his Father's kingdom; he knew well his Father's heart and intentions. On the night Jesus gathered his disciples together to lead them for the first time in what we now call the Lord's Supper, after serving the bread and wine and telling them the significance of the new covenant, he ended by saying he would not again drink of the fruit of the vine, until he could drink it with them in His Father's kingdom. This gathering was rooted in sincere worship and the joy of being in Jesus' presence.

Yes, the unthinkable was about to unfold, and for a while at least things were going to look pretty grim, but the end result, after Christ's resurrection and ascension, would be the

establishing of the gateway to eternal joy in the presence of
God.

To pray your kingdom come is to ask God to replace every
nook and cranny of your earthly being influenced by sin and
living under the influence of failure, flaw, displaced values, and
hopelessness, and through the regenerate work of Jesus Christ,
be filled with God's purity, will, and his desire while we are on
this earth. It means to pray for the culmination of all things and
the return of Christ to occur and the establishment of his
kingdom of complete purity and perfection forever.

All you have made will praise you, O Lord;
Your saints will extol you.
They will tell of the glory of your kingdom
and speak of Your might,
so that all men may know of your mighty acts
and the glorious splendor of your kingdom.
Your kingdom is an everlasting kingdom,
and Your dominion endures through all generations.[25]

Your kingdom come

Your Will Be Done

"We pray that we and all mankind may do the whole will of God in all things; and nothing else, not the least thing but what is the holy and acceptable will of God. We pray that we may do the whole will of God as He wills, in the manner that pleases Him: And, lastly, that we may do it because it is His will; that this may be the sole reason and ground, the whole and only motive, of whatsoever we think, or whatsoever we speak or do."[26]

Diversions come in two forms, planned and unplanned. When we plan a diversion we are usually ready or at least somewhat ready to accept the responsibility for whatever may unfold as a result of altering our original plan. That is because we are in the driver's seat, or at least that is what we want to think, but what about unplanned diversions where we aren't making the decision to change our course? What about the diversions we don't initiate and that are out of our control? Those produce different responses, like caution, doubt, discomfort, fear, and even anger. To state it plainly, most of us do not do well when things get out of our control.

For example, almost all young boys are adventurers, and growing up, my three sons were no exception. They enjoyed exploring, using their imaginations, and as a result, they often wandered out of the immediate yard when the opportunity arose. We didn't get overly concerned because they had 30 acres to roam on. Sure they could fall from a tree limb and break an arm; get stung by a wasp or get into poison ivy, but there was not much danger of abduction or a stray bullet from a drive by shooting. However, when they were small we always kept them somewhat close so we could get to them quickly if there was a need to.

One day when my sons were still very young and our house was under construction, I arrived home expecting to find the usual carpenters cutting and nailing lumber and finishing up the framework on the house and the boys playing in the yard in front of the mobile home we lived in while the house was being built. Dianna was probably inside preparing dinner with Benjamin, our 3 year old, or maybe even outside with all three boys playing.

Instead I drove up to see my wife with that very concerned mom expression on her face, and the construction workers searching the field, pond, and the woods around our house searching for our youngest son. As soon as I got out of the car she said, "We can't find Benjamin!"

The Vigil

I immediately began calling his name along with the others. Within seconds Benjamin appeared at the edge of the woods with a bewildered look on his face as he attempted to figure out why everyone was so frantically calling his name. In his mind he merely went for a little walk in the woods, no big deal.

Dianna had been outside with him and had no idea he would or could so quickly disappear into the trees. Benjamin had decided upon an innocent diversion and decided to head for the woods. He thought nothing of the possible ramifications of his decision or how it would affect others around him. Benjamin was okay because he had made his own diversion, but everyone else had varying levels of discomfort, concern, and fear because the situation was uncertain and out of their control.

Diversions can frustrate things because we like being in control of our environment and our future. Most of us are uncomfortable with change unless we initiate it, and if we're honest most of us want things done our way, period. That is why praying this part of the prayer does not come easily and sometimes is downright unsettling.

When we pray it sincerely, we are saying we relinquish control over our lives and we are trusting Jesus with our future. We are asking God to remove our desires and replace them with his. While we know that it is the right thing to pray, many perceive it as just too much of a risk.

We are concerned God may ask us to do something that is different than what we desire for the future of our lives. When we can't sincerely pray this part of the prayer, what we are really saying to God is, "I want to remain in control over my life and I am unwilling to surrender my plans to you."

No matter how quietly we might try to say it, it is still a brazen statement of rebellion against a God whose plans are never wrong or misguided. We are saying we don't trust God with our life and that our will is better than his will for us.

Reason should tell us that the Maker and Ruler of all creation, the most detailed being in existence, who loves us unconditionally, and who has fabricated his plans for us with meticulous detail, would be worthy of our complete trust, and thereby pave the way for a fearless future. But while we say we believe him to be the *Lord of all*, many discover inner conflict when it comes to saying, "Your will be done."

Is the struggle because we are not certain he really does have the ability to work all things together for our good, or is the struggle because we are willing to trust him for our salvation and our eternal future, but not the lesser choices we make on this earth between then and now?

Honesty forces the truth to be spoken, and the truth is, there are many who attend church that simply will not yield themselves or their plans to God, they simply don't care. Still others are not willing to position or quiet themselves before the Lord long enough to hear or see where He is leading and end up missing some wonderful things for their lives because life just got too busy with "stuff."

Then there are those who forge ahead asking God to bless them and whatever they do because they assume God exists to make certain their perception of life's best is given to them. Sadly though, should things turn south and difficult times and circumstances come, emotions fray and God gets blamed for something He never did or He is accused of unfilled expectations to which He never promised.

I believe there are others who are ready to obey the Lord's will, but find themselves like Paul in Acts chapter sixteen. His intentions were noble and kingdom minded, but as his journey to glorify God unfolded, he saw that not all he sensed he was to do lined up with the will of God, even though his motives were selfless.

With plans that were overridden by God, Paul found himself

confronted by unplanned diversions, at least from his point of view. Paul's response to diversion demonstrates how we are a vessel given over to the will of God. When he discovered his plans to be different than those of the designer of his destiny; he adjusted his plans and submitted to the will of his Maker.

In Acts 16 we see how Paul and his companions had planned to go to Asia to share the Gospel, but instead were prevented by the Holy Spirit from going for some undisclosed reason. Then, *"When they came to Mysia, they tried to go into Bithynia, but the Spirit of Jesus did not allow them."* Paul was not told why, only that he and his companions would not be allowed to go. During the night Paul had a vision of a man from Macedonia who was on his knees pleading for someone to come and help them.

They entered the region and after a few days found a location by the river where they would pray. In the process they happened along a group of women and began talking with them. It was during this time that a woman named Lydia heard their words and asked them for this salvation they were talking about. The result of this encounter resulted in her and her entire household becoming followers of Christ.

Sometime later as they were going along ministering, a

young woman, possessed by a demon, was constantly interrupting and bothering them. One day, Paul, tired of the distractions, turned to her and rebuked the spirit within her, and she was set free by the power of God. However, because of that event the slave girl's owners became angry with Paul. Why? Their source of making money from the slave girl's fortune telling ability was interrupted. The slave owners turned on Paul and his friends and caused them to be beaten and thrown into prison.

Why would God prevent them from entering one place only to have them land in jail in another? Human logic at this point might have deduced that somewhere God's will must have been missed, because things seemed to be less than favorable but that is the difference between our human perspective and God's heavenly one. What we see as an inconvenience, distraction or complete waste could actually be the best possible way for something to happen.

Time and time again in Scripture we see this happening, for example, what if Philip had not listened and gone out into the desert? What if he had lingered on the rational and reasonable, the fact that there was so much going on in Jerusalem he could be involved in. What if he had considered that there was nothing of any face value out in the desert that could possibly equal the opportunities waiting in Jerusalem and not continued to the Gaza road? It didn't make sense in the natural. How could he have known he would meet an Ethiopian eunuch who was one of such prominence and responsibility in his country? He wasn't told what was waiting ahead of him in the desert region, only that he should go. Fortunately, for the Ethiopian official and all who might have later been influenced for the kingdom of God, Philip obeyed God and fruit was born.

What if Jesus during his painstaking prayer in the Garden of Gethsemane had decided because of the impending humiliation, physical pain, and death, not to complete the task before Him because it didn't make sense in the natural? What if He after Peter had drawn his sword and cut the ear off the high priest's slave, actually called down those 12 legions of angel's He made mention of? Jesus passed by that defining moment earlier when He prayed *"My Father! If it is possible, let this cup pass from me. Yet not as I will, but as You will."*[27]

I have a friend who said to me once concerning the Garden of Gethsemane, "Can you imagine the angels looking upon this unfolding scene knowing how much the Father loved the Son, anxiously awaiting the signal from God to rush in and eliminate those who would harm God's son?" Yet the command did not come, because a flawless plan for the redemption of the world was in motion, even if no one but the Father knew how it would unfold.

Let's return to Paul's unplanned diversion and examine the results to see if it produced fruit for God's kingdom. Indeed, he and his travel companions were attacked by a mob, beaten, and thrown into jail, but they did an odd thing while they were sitting in a damp, musty cell. Around midnight they begin singing, but the spontaneous concert was interrupted by an earthquake that opened the cell doors and caused the chains that bound the prisoners to come loose. When the jailor realized what had happened, he prepared to kill himself because he knew he would be executed for allowing the prisoners to escape.

Before he could go through with it, Paul called out to him from the prison cell and told the jailor not to harm himself because no one had escaped, in fact no one tried. The jailor realized Paul was telling the truth and fell down at the feet of Paul and Silas. He actually escorted them out and asked them how he might be saved. The story ends with the fruit of a seeming diversion bringing salvation to the jailor and his entire household, an official apology from the magistrates, and the town's Christians giving glory to God.

If this were our story, most of us would probably not have written in the difficult section for ourselves to experience, and perhaps that is why God doesn't usually give a lot of future details to us because He wants us to trust Him, and to say, *Your will be done.*

Do you remember the story of Heather Mercer? She and her friend were captured and imprisoned by the Taliban while ministering in Afghanistan. They had been sharing the *Jesus* film with people in that Islamic war torn nation. While telling of their ordeal, she shared how frightened she was at times, but she also said one of the things she heard God ask her during her trouble was, "Will you trust me?"

Heather made it back home and because of her captivity and release, she has been given a platform to share her faith that she would not have had otherwise. The question Heather heard from the Lord, "Will you trust me?", is the question that leaves each of us with one of two responses. "Yes, your will be done", or "No God, my way is better".

I don't know about every Christian, but I have to be honest, I have not always enjoyed every moment of every ministry assignment I have had over the past three and a half decades. There have been moments of indescribable joy, fulfillment, and a feeling of valuable accomplishment for Christ and his Kingdom.

There have been plenty of occasions when I was tired and not spending enough quality time in God's presence that I would hope for a diversion in the form of a letter, e-mail, or phone call. Something that would invite me to a different assignment or at least a different place.

Fortunately when those times occurred I would stop and place myself in quietness before God and it wouldn't be long before wisdom would come through a trusted friend or a passage in the Bible and I would realize I was trying to create my own diversion, and those never produce the right fruit in the long run.

In a recent conversation I found myself responding to a question with an often-used phrase, "I don't know."

After 40 years of following Christ I find my love for him, level of trust in him and his unfolding plan higher and more exciting than ever, but I also realize the gulf that lies between me and my understanding of him is one of great breadth. I simply do not know why he does some things the way he does.

The Vigil

There are some things I have learned, but don't completely understand concerning God's will particularly displayed in the story of a shipwreck. I will tell you ahead of time that there are parts of this story, which disrupt my comfort zone and may disrupt yours as well. There is much leading up to the shipwreck that challenges shallow, feel good theology, but we cannot deny these stories exist in the Bible and that they are there for us to learn from, even if they bring discomfort to our cozy lifestyle.

The ship wreck is in the final two chapters of the book of Acts, but the events leading to it begin earlier during a farewell address given by the Apostle Paul in the city of Ephesus to his spiritual family there. He told them how much he valued them and all the Lord had done among them, but he continued to tell them that he must go to Jerusalem, even though he did not know his fate or the possibility of ever seeing them again.

Luke, who is narrating the story, said the emotions were so high at this point that they tore themselves from their friends as they boarded their ship. Later on one of the ship's stops, Paul's party visited the house of our friend Phillip the Evangelist where they were joined by a prophet named Agabus who told Paul he would eventually be bound in chains. Upon hearing this, not only did the people who heard this word beg Paul not to go to

Jerusalem, even his travelling companions tried to dissuade him. Paul however, said he was not only willing to be put in chains, but to even be put to death for the cause of Christ.

They continued their journey, and not more than three days later after entering Jerusalem a crowd attempted to kill him, and would have had they not been prevented by some soldiers from doing so. Shortly after that he was again confronted and rescued from an angry mob, followed by another situation where 40 men who took a vow not to eat or drink until they killed him. Paul experienced another series of trials and was shuffled from one place to another until he is finally placed on board a ship bound for Rome and an audience before Caesar.

The sailing voyage was met with bad weather and Paul approached his guard with information revealing a plan for their safe travel and arrival, but it was ignored. Pressing on against the warnings of Paul, the sailors encountered a more severe storm causing what appeared to be a tragic ending. Again Paul spoke up and told them an angel had appeared to him and assured him he would stand before Caesar, and that all those aboard the ship would survive if they followed his instructions.

They drifted at sea for 14 days before running aground on a sandbar. The waves began to break their vessel apart and all

The Vigil

aboard took to the water grabbing anything that would float. There were 276 people aboard, and they all safely reached the shore of an island called Malta.

What might disturb some is this question, why did the same God that could transport Phillip the Evangelist from a desert road safely to another place, not do the same thing for Paul?

Paul told the sailors what to do, but they didn't listen. Why was Paul subjected to the 14 days at sea in a storm, get shipwrecked, and then have to swim to shore? He was not the one disobeying, they were.

Was Paul subjected to this because he didn't have the right faith formula or revelation? I don't think so!

He may not have known each detail, but I don't believe difficulty was a surprise to Paul. After all, God shared with him shortly after his conversion how much he would suffer for Jesus sake. I don't like the word suffer any more than the next person, but if we attempt to remove it from the Bible we are going to end up with a much smaller book, filled with the plans of man, not the plans of God, and we are setting ourselves up for disappointment.

Human reasoning and manipulation will never lead to understanding the will and complexities of God. Only faith, trust, love, and obedience lead to relationship with Christ and accomplishing his will on earth as it is in heaven. That is why the road is narrow that leads to God, there are simply fewer people willing to pick up their cross and follow Jesus on his terms. This may sound hard, but it is nevertheless true.

Everything Jesus spoke while he walked the earth is powerful and right, everything written about in the Bible true, so it's difficult to list all my favorites, but these two are worth investing a long thoughtful pause before reading much further. Though brief, they are riveting to the human heart and God's cause.

The first was John's introductory remarks for his letter when he wrote, *"All things were created through Him (Christ), and apart from Him not one thing was created that has been created. Life was in Him..."*[28]

The second is when Jesus said, *"I have come that they may have life and have it in abundance."*[29]

Really, this is God's design for us? To understand that life doesn't exist outside him and that he wants us to have an abundant life? Attempting any self-designed will of our own reflects our shortsighted human nature. God, with no limits as to what he can do, wants us to experience an abundant life.

The Vigil

There is a verse, which has become a familiar friend to me over the years. I return to it whenever I feel restless or confused. I believe when it is read and prayed for help and guidance, God will honor the request.

Teach me to do Your will, for You are my God. May Your gracious Spirit lead me on level ground.[30]

Your will be done on earth as it is in heaven

Our Daily Bread

"The danger with the prayer for bread is that we get there too soon."[31]

I wish the story I am about to disclose were not true, but unfortunately it is. On one of my first multi-day prayer retreats years ago, I was very excited at the prospect of being alone to spend uninterrupted time praying, reading the Bible, and journaling my thoughts and prayers.

The destination for the retreat was a rustic log cabin in the Ozarks on top of a beautiful scenic mountain overlooking a waterfall pouring into a small canyon. As I made preparations I remembered one of the mottos from being in the Boy Scouts when I was young, *"Be Prepared"*. Since I had never stayed in this place before I wanted to make sure I had sufficient supplies for a prayer retreat.

I packed extra clothes; plenty of water, simple food items but plenty of them so I didn't have to leave the cabin or the top of the mountain it was located on. Since it was late fall I took some extra firewood for the cabin's old stone fireplace in case the weather turned cold. I took my Bible, journal, extra writing pads, a couple of books if I needed a change of pace, candles, and a lantern for the early morning praying and writing hours. Since I had planned to hike deeper into the woods during the day to pick a good quiet spot to pray and read that meant I needed my backpack and some hiking gear.

By the time I finished loading my small truck for the trip, there was hardly any room for me. Instead of a simple prayer retreat it resembled a small expedition to scale Kilimanjaro. Since that experience my prayer get-a-ways look a lot different, well okay, usually.

It must be human nature for most of us to want more than we need. When my sons were young and I would offer them candy from a bag or dish, they would usually not be content with just one handful. Ever wonder why some department store sales have to put up signs saying, "Limit one per customer"? I think that is because most of us tend to overdo it when it comes to what we think we need.

God is our Father in heaven, the Lord and ruler over all that exists and the directions that Jesus gave us stand in stark contrast to how we tend to over want things. As Jesus prayed concerning provision, he may have assumed it would be understood by all who were devoted to him, that in asking for our daily bread it meant to ask for those things necessary to fulfill his will for us while we on earth. To provide for today's necessities to carry out his will and work.

He can supply anything needed to facilitate his plans regardless of the economic situations governing our family or nations. He has sufficient resources to accomplish everything he desires and has called us to participate with him in accomplishing. There are no shortages, unbalanced budgets, or debt crises in his Kingdom. His coffers are self-sustaining and inexhaustible. We bear the weight of seeking and obeying his will, and in that place is where we often see the unmerited favor and the miraculous side of his ability to provide displayed.

While there are no limitations as to what he can do or provide we must also be careful to remember God in his inexhaustible qualities and abilities, is in no way indebted or bound to fulfill our personal whims, visions, or ideas. He is a loving, generous Father who blesses his children when and how he wants. However we should never think he is at our disposal to supply whatever we ask as though we were redeeming some sort of divine gift certificate when we recite a list of handpicked Bible passages. We owe him our lives, he saved us from certain destruction, and we are his servants, not the other way around.

Who then beyond God can know what we actually need to fulfill his will? Since he knows what we need better than we do ourselves, how could "Give us this day our daily bread" mean anything else except to request provision for the purpose of enabling us to fulfill the Father's heart for his creation?

Could it be interpreted this way? *Father please supply my needs for today so that I am able to move forward with the mission and message of Your kingdom.*

Our minds have been saturated with continuous marketing propaganda to condition us to follow a path of personal satisfaction and prominence and this mindset has unfortunately infiltrated many of those regularly attending church. Is it possible our context for provision has become a little skewed?

Compared to most of the world's living standards, many Americans live like royalty particularly when compared to the majority world. This is not an indictment or jab at anyone who enjoys the abundance of good things; merely a comment or suggestion for all of us to reconsider just what is really needed when it comes to material things. To occasionally stop to reflect and assess upon *how much is enough* and look to Scripture and ask God if our particular lifestyle has become excessive? Can genuine needs vary from person to person and according to the assignment God has given an individual or group? Of course.

I have some friends who lead a church in Manhattan. They needed a temporary space to meet while their permanent location was being completed. They approached the owners of a comedy club and offered them a way to earn additional revenue for their business by renting the space on Sunday mornings when it was not in use and they accepted. My friends were grateful to find a location for their services, but the rental was expensive. Property to both lease and purchase in the Manhattan region was and is astronomical even in a tough economy. For about a year I was travelling to and from Manhattan, staying a week each month to serve and assist them in their vision to plant a church in the Tribeca region.

During that season the possibility of actually transitioning our family there to live and minister became very real and my wife and I began the process of praying and weighing the challenges and adventure of such a move.

One day the pastor of the church scheduled an appointment with a realtor to view several housing possibilities, one of which was an apartment containing about 1,200 square feet of living space in a building on Warren just off Greenwich Street.

The Vigil

Granted it was nice with a great view of the area, but when we heard the price of the property I could barely believe my ears. The amount quoted as a *real deal* would buy 10 or 12 properties in our region of Arkansas.

However, if you are called to live in the region of Tribeca to live among its residents, to build friendships and relationships, to present Christ to them and build a genuine, caring community of Christian believers, it would be difficult to do it on the average church budget from Arkansas. What would be counted as extravagance in one area or situation may not hold true in another.

I have a new acquaintance, Rudy, who lives south of Manhattan, a little over 1800 miles south in fact. He resides in a small remote village in the jungle on the banks of a beautiful Central American river.

He is a native of the area, lives off the land, he is a lover of God, wants to serve the people of his village as a pastor, and though I'm sure given the opportunity he would like to improve his living situation some, his needs are vastly different from those of my friends in Manhattan. I had heard about Rudy moving from another part of Belize to pastor the new church through a friend in Belize Village2Village has helped support from time to time.

On my latest visit to the village where Rudy lives I got to meet the man we now all refer to as Pastor Rudy in person. He is an older man whose smile is infectious and seems to cover most of his face when he talks. I was with a team that had several trip objectives, one of which was to paint a simple rectangular shaped concrete block building constructed by the government several years ago to be used as a public school. We had painted it the year before, but didn't know the surface would not hold the particular paint we had used and so over the coming months and with the help of a hurricane, much of the paint flaked off. We felt we should return and do what was necessary to repaint the structure, which we did.

On the day we completed our part of the task, Rudy approached me, pointed to an empty five gallon plastic paint bucket and said, "My brother, may I have the bucket so I can clean it for gathering fresh rain water and on a hot day I can have a cool drink of fresh water?"

I told him of course, handed him the bucket and as he walked off toward the river to clean it out I thought about the few times over the years our city utility company had briefly turned the water off to our home in order to repair a main

The Vigil

waterline and how impatient I was until it was turned back on. I can get hot and cold water from several places in my house, and if it doesn't rain Rudy has to walk down a path to the river, fill up his five gallon bucket and then take it back to his house.

Need is quite different in each location, and God is aware of the conditions in each. He is able to meet the daily needs for those committed to his will in each place. The question is not whether God can supply our needs, but rather are we in the will of God? Because if we are, he has unlimited resource available to accomplish it.

The question is twofold:

- Are we positioned for him to provide our daily bread?
- Are we willing to be content with what he gives us to accomplish his will?

Our Father in heaven has no problem providing for us to do his will. If a morsel of food is needed to accomplish his work for the day, he can supply it, if his will for a particular thing requires the provision of food for an entire city, he can provide that.

On the opposite end of the village I just mentioned lives another man whose dwelling sits just a few feet from the river. His home is about the size of most lawn garden sheds in the backyards of many North American homes. His village was the first to be established in the country, there are only about 160 people who live there and all of its residents are very poor. The hurricane I mentioned that hit the region was not a huge one, but it sustained winds of 90 MPH and caused enough damage to create problems for those who already had their share of daily struggles and challenges.

In the last two years with the combined effort of a few churches from the United States, the village now has a small, well-constructed building to meet in for church services, visiting medical teams, and community gatherings. It was one of the few buildings that did not lose its roof in the storm and it is the place many of the residents gathered for refuge during and after the storm.

For my friend who lives on the riverbank and the rest of the people of the village, daily provision became even more difficult and complex after the storm. The damage assessment to repair the entire village came roughly to $25,000. (U.S. currency) about the price of an average vehicle in the United States, but in this poor Central American community it may as well have been a million dollars.

A couple of years ago a friendship began unfolding between

their village and a few US churches. From this friendship, medical teams and food has been sent, as well as construction assistance and other things to encourage the community. As a result of this friendship, some villagers have begun a relationship with Christ. I was even introduced to my first baptism where before the ceremony the area was checked for safety from crocodiles!

John and his family are missionaries who sacrifice and serve in this region fulltime and are originally from the same part of Arkansas in which I live. They ministered faithfully for more than a decade in a church south of our city, then a few years ago they took a short-term mission trip to the rural areas of Belize and that began a chain of events that eventually lead them to sell almost all they owned and move to the small community of Banana Bank on the Belize River where they have lived for more than four years.

They had just arrived in the United States to visit family when the storm just mentioned hit. John immediately returned as quickly as he could to evaluate the situation and though the damage was not devastating, there was still much loss. He returned again to the States and we all began praying for provision for the small village we have come to love.

The Vigil

Only a few days passed when he called me excited and in tears. Without him contacting anyone a lady he had met while ministering in a church in Alabama a year earlier, called and told him she would like to give a random financial gift to his ministry in Central America in the amount of $25,000. The *daily bread* needed in this situation was provided.

Often when stories like these are shared, questions arise:

- Is it wrong for Christians to have nice things?
- Is it wrong or a lack of faith to have health and life insurance?
- Is it wrong or a lack of faith to have savings and retirement plans?

This is just the tip of the, "How much is too much" iceberg, and we often define it by our particular lifestyle, but honestly I do think each of us could and should explore more seriously just how much is too much.

If we ask God he will tell us if we really want to know and his answer will vary from situation to situation and person to person. He has given us the Bible and the Holy Spirit to guide us.

The question and often the resulting internal tension is what we do with the information he gives us. Unfortunately it seems we often build our belief system and opinions around our desired lifestyle rather than building our lifestyle around the Bible.

Having material things is not wrong in itself, after all if we have a home of some sort, regardless of its size we would like something for guests to sit on when they visit, a table to eat from at meal times, storage space, and on the list goes. Materialism and excessiveness is not rooted in genuine provision, but when we are controlled by the desire for the newest, finest, biggest, and most expensive in unreasonable quantities, can the professing Christian really say Christ and his lifestyle is what truly rules them?

The word "moderation", *epieikes,* in its Greek form found in Philippians 4:5, *"refers to restraint on the passions, general soberness of living, being free from all excesses. The word properly means that which is fit or suitable, and then propriety, gentleness, and mildness. Paul the Apostle was telling Christians to not to indulge in excess of passion, or dress, or eating, or drinking. They were to govern their appetites, restrain their temper, and to be examples of what was proper for people in view of the expectation that the Lord would soon appear."[32]*

We could continue with many examples from my life or

yours, but let me propose this as the synopsis statement.

Satan's goal is to take the things which God has created for redeemed humanity to enjoy, and entices us to indulge in excessiveness, focusing on the elements and components for fulfillment and pleasure to the exclusion of the Creator and his purpose and boundaries for those elements and components.

I have heard numerous stories over the years of people who were living in a comfortable and secure environment, but suddenly found themselves in some situation which introduced doubt concerning their future, deposited seeds of worry, and caused insecurity to enter their lives. In fact I have walked with friends through some of these difficult situations as well as had friends walk with our family through similar situations.

Any number of things can enter our lives and change the landscape we're familiar with, and usually it is without the courtesy of an invitation or advanced notice. It can come in the form of a sudden job loss or failed business, dislocation resulting from a natural disaster, disappearance of financial security, or even in the form of a serious or debilitating illness.

Each time I have observed something like this occurring whether major or minor, there is an adjustment in the definition of what *needs* genuinely are. Provision is often defined or redefined by change in our circumstances. For instance we may think we have a legitimate need to buy a larger home, remodel a dated living room, buy a second car, and upgrade a three-year-old laptop. Then a tornado hits and provision is defined as a public shelter, a flashlight, and a jar of peanut butter.

Within hours of the news breaking of the Indian Ocean tsunami in 2004, a friend, one of my young heroes, was on his way to the southeast coast of India to assist in the relief effort. He reached his destination three days after the wave hit. The devastation and human carnage was beyond his ability to describe, must less understand, and the overwhelming need was mind numbing. Provision often was simply a smile and a cup of fresh water. In times like these the playing field is leveled and the essentials become the same for everyone, whether victim or rescuer.

I am not implying that faith in God is defined purely by living a simple life or in the midst of difficulty nor am I suggesting that wealth is evidence of a shallow spiritual experience. Most commentators agree though that the word bread used by Jesus in this prayer merely represents the request for the necessities for sustenance, for those things needed to accomplish His call, and is in no way a request for extravagance.

Most of us have seen footage of starving children in Africa, India, and Indonesia. I have personally seen people living in tiny, poorly constructed housing in Russia doing just about anything to stay warm and feed themselves and their families. I've also watched children in Mexican cities rummaging through city dumps for food, clothing, or something of value.

One night in New York City I was walking along a crowed sidewalk on Broadway with some friends when an employee walked out of a restaurant door with a large black trash bag of discarded food and scraps and placed it on the curb for pick up by the sanitation department. The bag no sooner hit the ground then a young man ran in from a dark corner some place, opened the bag, and began eating the food while stooping in the gutter. There wasn't even enough time to offer to help him before he grabbed all he could and again disappeared into a crowd.

The needs around us are overwhelming and can leave those desiring to help others wondering where to even begin. Now I understand many people experience lack because of wrong choices, others though could be in need because of something beyond their control or because of the greed, injustice, and indifference of corrupt systems and leaders.

I am not saying we are responsible for the irresponsible, that

The Vigil

we should support those who have a spirit of unearned or underserved entitlement or that we should all be equal in everything, but I do think we are quick to dismiss our responsibility when often it is within our ability to assist. "When it is in your power, don't withhold good from the one to whom it is due. Don't say to your neighbor, "Go away! Come back later. I'll give it tomorrow"—when it is there with you.[33]

While visiting a small village in Belize a few years ago with a team, one member of our party was giving away candy to the children. A young boy was trying to get more than his share of the candy and unwilling to take any if he couldn't get more than what was being offered. At first glance he seemed a bit selfish until we discovered his reason for wanting more was because he wanted to share with his siblings. He would do without rather than disappoint them.

My point is to appeal to those who embrace the word *Christian* as a lifestyle. To encourage each of us who call upon Christ as our Lord and Savior and approach him sincerely and ask how much is too much? I am in no way espousing socialism, but is it possible we are missing some important layers to the lifestyle of Christ that are also intended for those who follow him.

The sincere heart will hear a sincere answer from the one who loves us most, is concerned about us, and has perfect judgment and justice. He will give us what is sufficient for the task he has placed before each of us and he lead us to those we can help and freely give to as we have freely received.

Give us today our daily bread

Forgive us as we forgive

If we want to be like Jesus we have to forgive like Jesus.[34]

The sun had yet to rise high enough to break over the hill to the east, which would introduce the first rays into our little valley, but there seemed a greater amount of light filtering through the bedroom window than usual for this time of the morning. I slipped out of bed, took a few steps toward the window and slowly lifted a single slat on the blinds for a peek outside. Snow! Several inches of freshly fallen snow had covered the yard and everything in it.

Each branch of an old cedar tree outside was white and sagging under the weight of the wet snow, and it appeared as though someone had decorated it by hand. There was not a cloud in the sky so the sun accentuated the beauty of the new white landscape with an incredible brilliance. The snow even made our old run down shed look acceptable and hid the unsightly pile of aging lumber stacked next to it.

Two things made the day unique, first the Arkansas River valley doesn't see many snowfalls like this one, and secondly it was Christmas morning, a rare white Christmas. I grabbed my camera, went to the front door, stepped onto the porch and stood for several minutes gazing across the bright white field. The sun was beginning to cast a few subtle rays into the valley causing the snow's surface to glisten. There was a slight breeze, but apart from that the valley was almost completely motionless and filled with a wonderfully quiet calm.

Shivering because the temperature was twenty-three degrees, I couldn't bring myself to go back inside for some reason. I just kept staring at the beauty and enjoying the silence. Then slowly from behind a clump of cedar trees in the center of the meadow stepped three white-tail deer and I was able to get one camera shot off before they saw me and ran to the cover of some trees several yards away.

The newly fallen snow, the soft stillness, and the peace of an early Christmas morning seemed to offer a sense of purity and innocence, at least in one small valley on the edge of the Ozarks.

Interesting how snow can bring beauty to almost any landscape or item regardless of how old or new it is or how good or bad it may look the rest of the time.

Maybe that is why the Psalmist used it to illustrate the effect of God's grace on his heart when he wrote, *"Purify me from my sins, and I will be clean; wash me, and I will be whiter than snow."*[35]

We cannot eliminate the weight of our transgression or hide and remove its filth no matter how hard we try, but God can. He has a high and holy standard we are to live in honor of him for the world to see, and while I am not saying he won't remind us of our past should he see us drifting toward a destructive direction, he does that solely motivated by his love for us. He would never remind us of our past to embarrass or belittle us, and we who gather under the banner of Jesus would do well and be farther along in our pilgrimage in becoming Christ-like if we practiced forgiveness as Jesus forgives.

Not only does forgiveness cover over past transgressions, forgiveness is one of God's great power sources. It is an effective weapon against the plans of the enemy who ceaselessly attempts to separate us from the Father and as it is practiced forgiveness produces life, love, and freedom. His forgiveness is without prejudice and reinstates relationship without a list of unreasonable weights and unjustified demands.

When he sees a right and renewed heart, one which trusts in him, he responds with trust, not suspicion, unfairness, or unfounded penance. He does not shackle us with unreasonable burdens or place unloving and dry religious conditions upon us. In fact, you can usually recognize the forgiveness of God because it instills within the soul an indefinable freedom while removing condemnation and depositing a resolute desire to serve their liberator.

The world on the other hand tells us not to forgive, but instead to strike back, attempt to inflict harm, and demand repayment for wrongs and injustices. Is that what Jesus taught? Is that the example he displayed on earth?

The more I have tried to understand the power and depth of forgiveness, the more I realize the profound beauty of its divine design. I appreciate the benefits of its application and try to be a giver and distributor of this valuable and powerful commodity.

Genuine forgiveness, the forgiveness extended to us by God and required from him for us to extend to others, is a choice to make and a principle to follow if we are to live Christ-like lives

Jesus epitomized forgiveness as he entered Jerusalem for the final time. It was the beginning in a series of events that eventually led to his crucifixion and death. When Jesus rode into the city seated upon a humble donkey, he was greeted by crowds of people applauding and cheering him from each side of the city's narrow streets.

They were shouting his name, and honoring him as the long awaited Messiah. What an experience it must have been to stand shoulder to shoulder with so many of the city's curious and excited residents, drinking in the crowd's energy, as Jesus was being applauded and received by so many!

Have you ever wondered though if it were possible for Jesus to look into the faces of those that had laid palm branches and spread them out before him on the streets, who were shouting, *"Hosanna!"* and *"Blessed is he who comes in the name of the Lord!"*, knowing in a few days that many of those among the cheering fans would be calling for his death?

I think he knew some of the very faces that were affirming him as their hero and smiling as he entered the city would soon turn on him and be mocking, snarling, and trying to spit on him in disgust. Yet he continued. He knew what was unfolding. Here is the amazing part to me, he chose to forgive those who were about to inflict horrible injustices upon him even before they themselves knew they would turn against him.

The forgiveness of God is a quality and force that liberates the heart to pursue him in the greatest adventure life can offer and then eternity beyond. God forgives us for our transgressions against Him, and then He gives us the capacity to forgive others and as we do, we discover a level of freedom unattainable by human means.

However, when we choose not to ask forgiveness or to not grant forgiveness to those who have offended us we choose a yoke of slavery. Unforgiveness will spoil, darken, and decay our lives. We may say and even think we are free but we are not, and most others can see we're not either.

Like a dog restrained on a long chain, unforgiveness keeps us imprisoned and as long as we carry unforgiveness in our heart toward someone we might think we are free, but we are deceived. We can paint our chain blue, pink, or green, and spray it with the sweet scent of wildflowers, but the chain of unforgiveness is still present and holding us back.

We can talk and sing about freedom, say we are glad we are not like people outside the church, but we are still bound and limited, as unforgiveness strangles the life from us.

The person who is unforgiving is like the Pharisee in this parable of Jesus from Luke 18. *"Two men went up to the temple complex to pray, one a Pharisee and the other a tax collector. The Pharisee took his stand and was praying like this: 'God, I thank You that I'm not like other people—greedy, unrighteous,*

adulterers, or even like this tax collector. I fast twice a week; I
give a tenth of everything I get.' "But the tax collector, standing
far off, would not even raise his eyes to heaven but kept striking
his chest and saying, 'God, turn Your wrath from me —a sinner!'
I tell you, this one went down to his house justified rather than
the other; because everyone who exalts himself will be humbled,
but the one who humbles himself will be exalted."[36]

The Pharisee was blinded by his self-righteousness, he was the dog on the chain believing he was free, but he was the one bound, not the humble and repentant tax collector. I have been like that Pharisee before, and whenever God graciously reveals my unrighteous judgmental opinionated heart to me, I am grieved and broken at my filthy pride and shallow shortsightedness, ask for forgiveness, and thank the Father for grace and loving me enough to keep forming me into the image of Jesus.

Unforgiveness produces death, darkness, and a fruitless vine just as forgiveness brings life, light and the fruits of the Spirit. In my life I have witnessed and experienced both unforgiveness and forgiveness. Unforgiveness is a painful prison and the healing virtues of forgiveness are the freedom from that bondage. I have observed people who have chosen to forgive the seemingly unforgiveable and experienced a spiritual depth and freshness in Christ they previously thought was not possible.

I have also observed situations where people's lives were almost frozen in time and destined to remain in the shadows because they couldn't forgive even when the one who had offended them had asked forgiveness, repented of the infraction, and offered restitution.

Think of the emotional devastation and complete hopelessness that would occur if we had approached Christ with a repentant heart, asked forgiveness, only to have him respond with a cold, uncaring attitude of indifference and unforgiveness. It would destroy us, and indeed we would be without hope.

We are to forgive as he has forgiven us and there are no exceptions if we are to live as Jesus desires us to. I have heard it said, *"Unforgiveness is the poison we drink hoping others will get sick."* When we do not seek the path of forgiveness for our transgressions, or if we are unwilling to forgive others, we walk a bitter path and live a life far short of God's intended plan for us. Unforgiveness is an obstacle to real life and we cannot afford to ignore it and allow it to fester like an infection. It must be identified and extracted from our lives or our spiritual journey will be stifled and incomplete.

~

Several years ago I had a trip scheduled which I was really looking forward to with a lot of excitement, hope, and expectation. I was going to be gone for about two weeks and I had been carefully preparing for days. I packed the car the night before, set the alarm, and knew if I left by 7:00am I would arrive at my destination in Nashville around 4:00pm.

During the night a strong thunderstorm passed through our region. When I heard the wind and thunder, and saw the frequent intense lightening, I was worried it might knock out the electricity and I might over sleep, but it didn't.

Morning arrived, my alarm went off, I made coffee, showered, and quickly loaded the last few items needed into my small Ford Ranger, said goodbye to my family, I got in the car, put it in reverse, backed up a few feet in order to turn and head down the driveway. I then pulled forward about ten feet past a small work shed and began to make the sharp left turn down the hill then I quickly hit the brakes.

Stretching across the drive and extending twenty to thirty feet in both directions was a huge tree blocking my way out.

One of the largest oak trees on our property had been uprooted and blown over in the storm during the night and was completely obstructing any way of getting down the drive to the main road. I may have had good plans, provision for the trip, and been excited to go, but until the tree was dealt with, I wasn't going anywhere.

I could have closed my eyes and pretended the tree wasn't there, but that wasn't going to get rid of the problem. I could have blamed the storm for the tree falling and vow to never get into another storm, but that would not move the tree or stop future storms from coming either. I could blame the tree for falling, but that wouldn't remove the current obstacle either. I had to deal with removing the obstacle in front of me!

I trudged back into the house, changed clothes, got the chainsaw and ax from the shed, and for the next hour or so worked and cut until there was a passage through the fallen tree to continue my journey.

Some attempt to deal with unforgiveness in their life like I was tempted to with the tree. They blame others, look down on them, and select who and how they will forgive as defined by them, instead of by God. If we refuse to deal with the obstacle rightly and simply turn a different direction pretending it is not there more often than not the problem just gets worse.

Often unforgiveness is a sign of an unhealed wound picked up somewhere along life's path. If we do not deal with it, ask God for the grace to really forgive, the bitter root grows manifesting in constant suspicion, distrust of others and insecurity. Left unattended, the spirit of unforgiveness wounds others and keeps spreading.

Unforgiveness is an obstacle that prevents us from moving forward into the place of fruitful productivity for the Kingdom of God and thus our own welfare. Unforgiveness is spiritually debilitating. We may think we are doing good, living life, but the truth is as long as there is the obstacle of unforgiveness in us we will never know the optimum experience the Lord wants us to have.

Healing and health come when we forgive as Jesus forgave. Within forgiveness is the depth and wealth of liberty, surpassing all other human experiences, it is the threshold to knowing love's zenith.

The stories of innocence suffering at the hands of injustice are sad and all too numerous in this world and were it not for the healing mercy of God intervening and the application of his life principles moving in our lives, we would remain in a place of devastating hopelessness.

Some years ago, a man I have walked with for more than 18 years told me of an event that took place in his early childhood leaving deep emotional scars for many years.

The event took place on a Christmas morning when he was 14 years old. He was looking forward to a family day of fun; opening gifts from under the Christmas tree, laughing, exchanging stories, and eating the traditional holiday meal. Early in the morning his dad put on his coat and told his son he was going to the store to pick up a few things and that he would return home quickly. He asked his father if he could ride along with him to the store, but his dad said no. Though young, he sensed something was not right as he watched his dad walk out the door and out of his sight. That was the last time he saw his father until many years later when he was a grown man.

Was that fair?

Was it right?

What kind of wounds and obstacles did that incident cause? He told me after sharing that story, that as a husband and father himself now, he had no constructive, fatherly life lessons to use from of his younger years with his dad as an example to apply to his own children. He had no first-hand experience of what a functional family looks like or the knowledge and feeling of what it is like to have a father present in the home providing guidance, protection, and most importantly, love.

His years have been riddled with rejection, confusion, instability, distrust, untruths, crime, and years of abusing himself in attempts to temporarily escape his memories. He still struggles with forgiving himself for some of his past actions, and thus has a difficult time believing God would forgive him. When he fully understands the quality of Christ's forgiveness and walks in it, he will have the power to not only forgive himself and others, but he will also discover a new strength, joy and freedom.

Our being forgiven is inseparable from our ability to forgive others who have offended us, but can that possibly be Biblical?

"The key to understanding (Jesus) teaching is to recognize that we do not receive forgiveness without forgiving others, but because we cast ourselves on the mercy of God. Yet we cannot receive forgiveness without forgiving others. The man who mouths the words 'Forgive us our debts,' but will not forgive others their debts, has not begun to understand the weight of his own sin. If he did, in the light of it being forgiven, he would be prepared to forgive his brother 'seventy-seven times' (Matt.

18:22)"[37]

There are two more places in the Bible we should visit before the closing of this chapter, because they display a level or quality of God's forgiveness almost beyond comprehension. Yet if we are to be like Christ and effectual as He was, then we must yearn for this quality of forgiveness to flow from us as well. This is the first,

"Two other men, both criminals, were also led out with him to be executed. When they came to the place called the Skull, there they crucified him, along with the criminals — one on his right, the other on his left. Jesus said, "Father, forgive them, for they do not know what they are doing." And they divided up his clothes by casting lots. The people stood watching, and the rulers even sneered at him. They said, "He saved others; let him save himself if he is the Christ of God, the Chosen One."[38]

How did Jesus do this? How did he find the strength to pray a prayer of forgiveness while in the hands of his executioners? He was dying; he had done nothing wrong deserving of the heinous torture being inflicted. He could have called down fire to consume those responsible, but he didn't. And, does he actually expect us to respond the same way should some gross injustice be thrust upon us? I think yes.

Here is the background for the second passage worthy of our attention. We are about to hear the final words of a man just before he dies. Was he a thief, murderer, rapist, a despicable human-trafficker? No, in fact he was known to have a good reputation in the city that he lived, his fellow church members recognized him as one being full of the Spirit, wisdom, and faith. He was a leader in his church; full of the grace of God and displayed spiritual power, which he freely used to minister to the people he served.

Like Christ before him, he was confronted by people who were steeped in religion, plagued with jealously, wrong motives, and filled with anger against him. Their desire was for him to be silenced and disappear. They methodically stirred up a crowd with lies about him and dragged him before a religious council.

When he was asked by the council to give an account for the accusations against him, he merely used the stories from their shared religious history to reveal Jesus as their long awaited Messiah, but instead of them recognizing and receiving him as such, they instead crucified him becoming betrayers, murderers, and breaking the very law God had entrusted them with.

This didn't play very well before this audience and they went ballistic. Enraged with anger they dragged him out of the city and once there they began to cast stones on him to kill him.

Now enters the near incomprehensible. During the process of this horrific injustice, Stephen called upon the Lord and said, *"Lord Jesus, receive my spirit!" Then he knelt down and cried out with a loud voice, "Lord, do not charge them with this sin!" And saying this, he fell asleep."*[39]

Do not charge them with this sin?

Astounding!

Most would be crying for justice and retribution. How is this possible? How can we, how can anyone, forgive such atrocity and unfairness?

As it happens I'm writing today from a 14' x 20' cabin located at a ministry headquarters in Banana Bank, Belize.

The only sound that I have heard for a while is that of tropical birds and some monkeys in the distance. My quarters are humble, but relaxing and peaceful. The last thing I want to think about is somebody breaking in, dragging me outside and throwing rocks at me until I am unconscious or dead, and I am not sure I would go peacefully. Actually, I'm not certain how I would respond at all, let alone if I'd respond peacefully. How should we respond in any situation where we are being offended or abused in some way?

A closer examination of the passage reveals God's provision of strength, the grace that enabled Stephen to both know how to respond and endure the horrible situation. Stephen was, *"full of the Holy Spirit, he gazed intently into heaven and saw the glory of God; and Jesus standing at the right hand of God..."* Stephen was full of the enabling power of the Holy Spirit. His gaze was on God and His glory. We don't know how we would respond or endure things like this; we can't even wrap our minds around it, but we can know the same source as Stephen. The one who has promised that if we seek him, love him, trust him, we will not be disappointed.

This is what we know about forgiveness:

- If we want to be like Jesus, we have to love like Jesus.
- If we want to be like Jesus we have to love what Jesus loves.
- If we want to be like Jesus we have to forgive like Jesus forgives.

"Failure to forgive one another wasn't a matter of failing to live up to a new bit of moral teaching. It was cutting off the branch you were sitting on. The only reason for being Kingdom people was that the forgiveness of sins was happening; so if you didn't live forgiveness, you were denying the basis for your own new existence."[40]

"For if you forgive people their wrongdoing, your heavenly Father will forgive you as well. But if you don't forgive people, your Father will not forgive your wrongdoing."[41]

In Mark chapter 11 Jesus talks about a simple fig tree, a story which as with many in the Bible contains several levels of principles for us to glean from.

Jesus was travelling with his companions and was hungry. He saw a fig tree in the distance, but as he got close to it found it not only without fruit, but not even bearing any edible buds and evidence of fruit to come which would have been the norm for that season. Apparently it was covered in leaves and looked good like the other fig trees, but it was void of fruit or any signs of producing any. He then cursed the tree within earshot of the group saying, *"May no one ever eat fruit from you again!"[42]*

One early morning sometime later they were again passing the same way and happened upon the same tree when one of the guys saw it and remembered Jesus cursing it and brought it to Jesus' attention. Jesus immediately began to share with his disciples that with the right faith they too could do such things. He told them what to do, they had to pray, they had to ask, and they had to believe, and it would come to pass.

Then he added something very interesting and significant for us to hear and to respond to rightly if we discover the violation in our own lives. He said if during the praying, asking, believing process we find unforgiveness in our lives toward someone else, we should forgive that person just as the Father in heaven has forgiven us. If we do not forgive as the Father has forgiven, then neither will the Father forgive us.

I don't claim to be a great scholar but I do know this, just hanging out in the orchard doesn't assure you are producing fruit and evidently the owner and caretaker of the orchard is looking for fruit or he doesn't consider you a real tree. The other principle revealed in this parable is that unanswered prayer could very well be linked to unforgiveness.

From a distance the barren fig tree appeared to be a source of nourishment, but closer examination revealed the absence of fruit for nourishment or hope of any in the future. Likewise, religion understands the information of forgiveness, but falls short of necessary and sincere application. The result could cause the appearance of life, but void of the actual fruit to produce it.

The devastation caused by unforgiveness can be catastrophic; and the power, scope, and liberty of forgiveness immeasurably good, so then, to be like Jesus we must choose to forgive as the Father has forgiven us.

Forgive us our debts,
as we also have forgiven our debtors

Lead us not into temptation

"Gethsemane suggests the deepest meanings of the prayer: 'Do not let us be led into the Testing, but deliver us from evil.' Again and again Jesus says to his followers: watch and pray that you may not enter into temptation." Jesus knew, "that he must go, solo unaided, into the whirlpool, so that it may exhaust its force on him and let the rest of the world go free. And his followers must therefore pray: Let us not be brought into the testing"[43]

Almost every Bible translation introduces Matthew chapter four with the heading, The Temptation of Jesus. It is not part of the inspired Scripture; it is just a section heading to let the readers know what is coming up. Then unfolds the details of how Jesus was led by the Spirit into the desert to be tempted by the devil. A couple of chapters later though in his prayer for his disciples and our model prayer as well we find Jesus saying, "And lead us not into temptation"

The Bible isn't contradicting itself when it says, "God is never tempted to do wrong, and he never tempts anyone else.[44] Yet Jesus seems to say in this section of his prayer, "Pray that God doesn't lead you into temptation" It does seem a little perplexing at first.

I love words; to me the world would be pretty boring

without them. They are often abused, misapplied, scarce, or overused, but we have them so we can communicate. There are times when some words or phrases can only mean one thing and other times they appear to have more than one meaning.

Take the word *light* for instance. In the English language it can refer to something that is the opposite of darkness, or it can mean something that is the opposite of heavy. The meanings of the two words are defined by their context, like this sentence, "The light over the table revealing the contents of the room is light enough in weight to hold with two fingers." It is the same word, yet it is defining two very different things in the sentence.

Years ago I attended a weekend retreat with a group of guys that was held in a big rustic dorm at the top of White Rock Mountain in Arkansas. One of the guys who attended was in his early teens, and had recently moved from Vietnam and understood very little English. No one could seem to properly pronounce his name, so he asked us to simply call him Bobby.

The room for sleeping contained about twenty bunk beds with the only light for the room being a single 75 watt incandescent bulb hanging from the ceiling in the center of the room and turned on and off by pulling a long white string hanging from the side of the fixture. The evening was coming to a close, and everyone was in their bunks, except our new Vietnamese friend.

I recall one of the other men saying to him from his bunk, "Hey Bobby would you catch the light?" The next thing that happened was our Asian brother quickly jumped to the middle of the room and positioned himself under the fixture to rescue it before it came crashing to the floor. After a couple of seconds he realized, "catch the light" meant only to turn it off by pulling the string which he quickly did and climbed into his bunk.

While that is a humorous example, there can be more complicated results when words and phrases are not properly understood.

I have a friend who has a human resource position for a large corporation in the United States that was sold to non-English speaking investors. Part of his assignment was to explain and interpret some of the corporation's benefits for employees, guidelines, and company programs and provisions to the new owners. The process of integrating two different cultures with two different languages and systems presented more challenges than he had anticipated.

After days of communication via e-mails and phone calls concerning employee retirement programs, he realized the new

The Vigil

owners did not understand what a 401k was, even though they indicated in earlier conversations that they did. Without clarification they could have assumed 401k was a machine part or a room on the fourth floor of the plant.

The problem was not intelligence or a lack of words, but each understanding the other's language. Even though they used interpreters, some words still needed further clarification because they simply meant something different on the other side of the world.

In the mid-eighties I took a trip to Australia. I landed in Melbourne, met my hosts and proceeded to their car. As we walked up to his vehicle, he said, "Just toss your grip in the boot." I had no idea what the guy was talking about, and we both spoke English, I just stood still until he clarified, "Oh - uh, put your luggage in the trunk." Ahh, that time I understood.

Understanding the intent and context of certain words and phrases is vital for language to accomplish an actual communication exchange and provide adequate information to proceed onward.

Using this premise, a glance at this passage may appear perplexing, but there is no contradiction taking place in these statements in the Bible concerning temptation, they are not in opposition.

There is no language confusion, at least from God's perspective and His is the one that really counts.

God did not say one thing and then change His mind about it later. Jesus was led into the desert to be tempted by satan, but he didn't yield any of his purity, holy principles, or righteous characteristics in the process of what unfolded. He returned from his desert experience and the encounter of temptation by the evil one, without compromise or stain.

He led a sinless life on earth, was falsely accused of crimes he did not commit, subjected to cruel and inhumane treatment and then killed. Before any of this began though, these were his words during his prayer time in the Garden of Gethsemane. *"He prayed that, if it were possible, the awful hour awaiting him might pass him by. "Abba, Father," he cried out, "everything is possible for you. Please take this cup of suffering away from me. Yet I want your will to be done, not mine."*[45]

He was not granted reprieve from the ordeal because it was the will of the Father for Jesus to disarm the powers of darkness benefiting all of mankind. Jesus was not delivered from the intent of evil, at least initially.

He endured the tribulation and when Christ overcame the

The Vigil

power of the grave, he rose from the dead the unscathed victor, and provided all of humanity with a way to escape the ultimate plan of the evil one. Through the power of his redemptive work Jesus enabled all who would follow him the ability to be led away from temptation. Christians do not have to give into it.

The privilege and emphasis here is on the leading aspect. Lead us away from that which would harm and destroy us, and lead us God in your way instead.

- Ps 5:8 "Lead me, O Lord, in your righteousness."
- Ps 23:2 "He guides me in paths of righteousness for his name's sake."
- Ps 25:5 "You guide me in your truth and teach me"
- Ps 27:11 "Teach me your way, O Lord; lead me in a straight path"
- Ps 31:3-4 "Since you are my rock and my fortress for the sake of your name lead and guide me. Free me from the trap that is set for me, for you are my refuge."
- Ps 61:2 "lead me to the rock that is higher than I."
- Ps 73:24 "You guide me with your counsel."
- Ps 139:24 "lead me in the way everlasting."
- Ps 143:10, "lead me on level ground." [46]

On a V2V mission trip in Central America to a village called More Tomorrow, one of the assignments of our team by local missionaries required a large hose to be stretched a couple hundred yards from the village through dense tropical brush and a bamboo thicket down to the river in order to pump water into the village for a construction project. A narrow path was cut by hand with machetes by a couple of the villagers to the riverbank. In places along the narrow trail the brush was so thick the cuttings created more of a tunnel effect then an actual path.

None of our team ventured into the newly cut path from the clearing to the river the first day. One reason was because of the warnings we had received regarding one type of snake that had the reputation of being the seventh most dangerous and venomous in the world. In fact I met a dear lady named Delores whose husband had been bitten by one of these snakes and died.

Another reason was the path had been cut through an abundance of a tall bamboo like bush with sharp needles that caused extreme pain and muscle cramping if it pricked the skin.

On the second day in the village my curiosity to see the riverbank at the end of the newly created path won out and I approached one of the two men who had cut the path and asked if he would lead me to the river. I knew of his reputation and skills in the bush, familiarity of the area, and felt comfortable with his keen eyes to spot and avoid any danger. We hiked through knee high grass, then chest high grass, before disappearing into the bush.

After 100 yards or so the beauty of the river appeared, and after a few minutes we returned to the clearing. After I returned two other members of the team asked if it was safe, and I said, "Sure!" and off they went until they disappeared in the thicket. I returned to the river along the narrow passage way three or four more times that day.

On one of the trips while gazing at the beautifully clear running river, I heard someone making their way through the jungle and when the person finally appeared it was one of our younger female team members exploring alone. Fear along that particular path was now greatly diminished, and so was our ability to brag about our adventurous spirit into danger.

When we follow Christ's leading, trusting him for guidance and the resources to overcome the evil one, we will not find ourselves giving into temptation. He knows the path through the thicket to the beauty of the river.

"Perhaps we could paraphrase the whole request in this prayer as 'Do not allow us to be led into temptation that overwhelms us, but rescue us from the evil one'. So behind these words that Jesus gave us to pray are the implications that the devil is too strong for us, that we are too weak to stand up to him, but that our heavenly Father will deliver us if we call upon him."[47]

And lead us not into temptation

Deliver Us From Evil

"I will fear no evil, for you are with me"[48]

The night I began writing this chapter our region was under a severe thunderstorm watch for the fifth night in a row, the result of a stalled front across the Southeastern United States. However, on this evening all I could hear outside my window was a gentle spring shower and the very faint sound of thunder far in the distance, nothing resembling a storm threat.

Suddenly there was a bright flash of light that filled the room, accompanied by an almost simultaneous loud crash of thunder that shook the entire house and caused my adrenaline level to shift from a gentle hum to a frenzied screech in a split second.

The lightning was brash, unexpected, and demanded my attention, I sat frozen for a few seconds, but then I dismissed it as nothing to really be overly alarmed about. However, at the peak of the experience, it was very unnerving.

Fear is interesting because something that might bring worry or even terror to one person may hardly receive a second glance at all from another. If we are the one in the middle of something scaring us, it is very real to us regardless if someone else is frightened or not. If the fear source continues without change and unchallenged it can potentially victimize and eventually debilitate us. Fear is satan's primary tool of intimidation, he cloaks it in lies and deception, and he finds it useful and effective to distract us from God.

In the late 1950's, in an old neighborhood on the west side of town, down a narrow street bordered on each side with mature trees, sat a small, one bedroom home where a family of four lived.

The house had a basement one half of which had been finished as a room for people to gather, while the other side still contained the original concrete floor and old cement block walls. In the dimly lit unfinished portion sat a workbench, some storage items, a washer and an old coal furnace that heated the house.

A few feet from the furnace behind a wooden plank door was a small, unlit room used as a coal bin that held a large pile of coal chunks to fuel the furnace and heat the house in winter. On the outside wall of the coal room was a small square heavy cast metal door which could open to the outside when the coal company would periodically deliver the dusty black fuel by shoveling it through the door into the coal room. The metal door to the outside was always kept locked except on coal delivery day.

One evening a young boy found himself having to go down to the basement to retrieve something from the unfinished side, the side with the dark coal bin. Though there really wasn't a good reason for fear, he still never liked going down into the basement by himself at night, so as he approached the door at the top of the stairs leading down to the basement, he began to feel himself tense up.

He opened the door and quickly reached for the switch that would light the stairwell and the finished side of the basement. Once everything could be seen he began to descend the steps, and as each one led him further down into the basement, he cautiously peered between the board slats along the left of the stairway, which gave him partial view into the room below while he hugged the wall and handrail to the right.

Reaching the landing he made two final steps down to the left and entered the room. Crossing the black linoleum tile floor and approaching a second sliding pocket door which led into the poorly lit unfinished side of the basement, his emotional

The Vigil

intensity grew as he reached for the handle and slowly slid the door open. He always wondered why there wasn't a switch on the entrance side of the door, why make a guy stick his arm into the darkness for something to grab it.

He carefully moved through the second door, he could now see his dad's workbench. Approaching the bench he kept his eyes trained on the old wooden door leading into the blackness of the coal room. He could feel his fears growing. Suddenly this thought jumped into his mind, "What if someone or something got into the room through the unlocked delivery door to the outside?" Did he just hear a sound, a squeak from inside the coal room?

The boy quickly grabbed the tool off the bench and began a quick retreat through the door dividing the two rooms, not taking time to shut it, then making a dash for the stairs and up to safety. That's when the unthinkable happened. He heard the creak of the old wooden coal room door as it drug across a high spot on the concrete floor. He broke into a full sprint, jumped over the first two steps and turned on the landing for the quick ascent away from whatever was emerging from the coal room.

Halfway up the steps with the safety of the door just ahead, he felt a brief sense of relief when suddenly from between the gaps in the wood slats a huge hairy arm shot through two of the boards and attempted to grab the his leg.

"HELP!!" he shouted as adrenaline shot through his body like a lightning bolt and he hugged the opposite wall trying to put as much distance as he could between him and the arm while still running and leaping up the stairs like a frightened gazelle pursued by a hungry leopard.

That's when I bolted to a sitting position on my bed with my eyes wide open and my heart pounding in my chest. This was a nightmare, a dream, but all too real! It was an often-repeated nightmare that always yielded the same response, a near paralyzing fear. With eyes wide open, I would pull my arms, legs, and head under the bed covers until I could finally fall back to sleep. When I would later get up out of bed, I would make sure there was more than an arm's reach of room between me and anything that might still be waiting under my bed.

As a very young boy, that dimly lit basement and coal room was pretty intimidating, especially at night. I don't know where the fear came from initially; I just know to me it was a problem. On several occasions while wide awake and not dreaming I would leave that old basement running up those stairs hoping to make it to the top and close the door before whatever was

The Vigil

sparking my imagination had time to develop into real substance. Deliverance from what I perceived as "unknown evil" was all I wanted.

Fear, deception, and intimidation are weapons of the evil one against us. If we don't take action against him, he uses those tactics very effectively to derail us from God's plans and intentions. Fear is very real and manifests in a variety of ways and forms.

Fear of the dark, fear of heights, fear of water, caves, animals, disease, change, losing a loved one, losing a job, losing a position or respect, fear of the unknown, uncertainty, and to some, in-laws and even the IRS.

What does our heavenly Father have to say about fear, particularly as it pertains to those who position themselves under his care? He says emphatically, *"Don't be afraid, for I am with you. Don't be discouraged, for I am your God. I will strengthen you and help you."*[49]

Stating it plainly, there is a place in Christ that we do not take advantage of, while he tells us to not be afraid, many Christians including myself, often are. May God help us to wisely increase our level of trust in him, which really means relinquishing our control.

We aren't alone in the need of increasing trust in Jesus, it began with his own disciples as they were travelling alongside him and learning to be like him and minister like him.

On one occasion Jesus' disciples had observed yet another unexplainable event performed by him when he fed well over 5,000 with five loaves and two fish. When the meal was over and those who had known of the overwhelming problem of insufficiency to accommodate the crowd with the small amount of food on hand saw the satisfied and well-fed crowd, they had to have been amazed by the transformation to sufficiency. Nothing less than a miracle had taken place, a big one, and the disciples knew who had performed it, but watch what unfolds as the story continues.

After the meal Jesus instructed his team to get into a boat and row to the other side, while he dismissed the crowd. They did as he said while he went away to a mountain to pray.

As they crossed the sea the weather turned rough; they were straining at the oars to get their boat to the other shore. Around three in the morning Jesus went walking by on the water, and according to Scripture he had intended to pass them by, but when he saw their fear he came to their aid. *"Have courage!"* he said, *"It is I don't be afraid."* [50] and after he spoke to them he climbed into the boat and completed the journey with them.

Earlier they had witnessed the miraculous feeding of the huge crowd with only enough food for a few people and even at that number a fish sandwich would have been really light on the fish. What a faith builder that must have been to his disciples!

Don't you think the topic of conversation among them as they began their trip was probably filled with emotionally charged comments about what unfolded as they verbally relived the event? I bet it would have been potentially difficult to get a word in initially because they were so excited. I know I would have been.

Why would they be fearful now after just witnessing such an extraordinary display of God's ability to change the seemingly unchangeable? Maybe it was because they weren't in any personal danger from the hungry crowd, but now they were in a different situation altogether, which required a different application of faith. Maybe it was because Jesus wasn't with them in the boat. I can certainly understand why they might have had questions like:

Why did he send them out so late in the day?

Why not have them wait until the next morning to begin

their trip?

Why didn't he accompany them?

On a boat at night in stormy seas they thought they had very valid reasons for fear or *deep concern* to quote an oft-heard phrase. A phrase that is a religious politically correct term we choose to cloak our fear with to avoid drawing fire from those who might say, "Where is your faith?" Since Jesus wanted to pass them by he evidently wasn't concerned about their situation being permanently or overwhelming destructive.

Is it possible he intentionally sent them into the situation to strengthen their trust in God for future endeavors that would require even more faith and trust?

Could he have wanted them to trust him for deliverance from the storm with the same miraculous ability he had just displayed to them by providing food for well over 5,000 people just hours earlier?

Was he attempting to show them he didn't have to be physically present to provide and perform the miraculous to facilitate His will for those following him?

I don't know, but how often have we experienced God's favor, protection, or provision in some way and yet yielded to concern or fear shortly after to a new change in circumstance?

I know I have.

We get intimidated by things we can't stop or control, and that's why the evil one uses fear to throw us off balance, hoping to get us to forget that as Christians we are under the watchful care of the Maker of all that exists! Our Father in heaven tells us to seek him with all our heart, devote ourselves to him, and do not fear anything except him.

In Psalm 56 verses 3 and 4, written by David in the context of his evasion of Saul's attempts to kill him that says, *"When I am afraid I will trust in You. In God, whose word I praise, in God I trust; I will not fear. What can man do to me?"*[51]

The evil one and his evil exist, and his goal is to kill, steal, and destroy, he hates God and he hates us. The Bible says the Spirit of God that exists within the repentant believer in Christ Jesus is greater than the evil one who would try to harm us, and that is the truth we must embrace. We should not fear satan, but we should realize he is an experienced fighting foe and been around a long time fine-tuning his craft of evil.

We have the comfort of Scripture that tells us the battle belongs to the Lord, and the devil is no match for the power of God. That is why we must love and trust God alone, for without him we are hopeless prey to the darkness and can fall victim by our own choices to eternal separation from God.

Be on guard, but do not fear! With Jesus Christ as our Lord, Savior, Mediator, and Protector, we have nothing to be afraid of, and are actually more than conquers according to God's Word!

My prayer is not that you take them out of the world but that you protect them from the evil one.[52]

The Lord is my light and my salvation — whom shall I fear? The Lord is the stronghold of my life — of whom shall I be afraid?[53]

But deliver us from the evil one

The Vigil

The Doxology

"Our Lord and God, You are worthy to receive glory and honor and power, because You have created all things, and because of Your will they exist and were created."[54]

Jesus began this most remarkable prayer model by exalting the Father in heaven, and thereby revealing humankind's highest duty, privilege, and call. Jesus' words in Matthew 6:9-13 are the divine archetype for vigilant prayer and a spiritually vigilant life upon this earth. He closes with a climactic doxology to finish honoring the only one worthy and deserving of it.

Try as I might to use human language to express gratitude, recognition, and the honor due the Creator God Yahweh, my attempts are feebly insufficient. I don't think I'm alone in this attempt though. Have you ever felt overwhelmed as you try to express worship, honor and gratitude to our God?

The Psalmist David repeatedly throughout his writings used poetic language to honor the Lord of heaven and earth and more eloquently than anyone, in my opinion, exhorts everything that has breath to praise the Lord. As he encourages us to give the glory that is due God, even declares himself,

"*Hallelujah! Give thanks to the Lord, for He is good; His faithful love endures forever.*

Who can declare the Lord's mighty acts or proclaim all the praise due Him?"[55]

On this side of heaven who can properly present to God all the worship due him? The prayer began in acknowledgement and adoration of our heavenly Father, moved next to his intention of his kingdom rule and will to saturate everything with his glory.

Jesus presented the invitation for us to request of God the daily provision needed to accomplish our divine assignment. Following that is the emphasis on forgiveness, which is the qualifier and catalyst for relationship with him and others.

He moves to asking for help in evading the schemes and devices of darkness and introduced us to petitioning for his leading us toward righteousness and the deliverance from the evil one. Closure comes where the prayer began, in abandoned exaltation to the indescribable God of all creation.

All we can see, access, and comprehend, directs us to reflect on the beauty, majesty, and operation of God's broader kingdom. His kingdom stretches beyond us into the supernatural realm.

On the earth are numerous animate and inanimate displays of his inexhaustible ingenuity and immeasurable ability.

Some of those things cause us to respond in silence and awe. Some cause our eyes to tear up like when the birth of child occurs.

If we think about it even the bodily reactions that take place in order to produce a single tear is a miracle of God's design in and of itself.

Whatever the experience, even the earth's best offering is still frail and disappointing compared to what awaits the Christian in our future eternal existence. Worship is our call and valued privilege, but at its best here on Earth it is still a dim reflection of things to unfold when we finally arrive in his heavenly presence. Even though we can delve into worship's depths or soar to its highest heights here on earth, those places are still but a mere taste, an antithesis, compared to beholding his glory in heaven.

In the jungle on the bank of the Belize River is the village named More Tomorrow that I mentioned earlier. Since it is the oldest village in the country, the first few times I heard someone say the name I thought it was perhaps an ancient Mayan word, and I even wrote it down as, *Mortamaro* and wondered what deep meaning the name contained.

Later though I discovered it was not mysterious, simply More Tomorrow. I asked a couple of the villager's its origin and no one really knew except for the obvious, which was, *what we don't have time today to do there will be...more tomorrow.*

One night in the newly established church there about 30 people gathered for a worship service. I was asked to lead so I grabbed my guitar and began to sing a couple of choruses I was told the villagers knew. The first few seconds into the song revealed to me that I was definitely not in the States in a facility with a state of the art sound system and first call musicians.

This was not the well-rehearsed polished presentation often experienced in many Western churches. The added ambiance was not facilitated by the latest technology and multi-media presentations designed to enhance our senses, but heat, humidity, insects, nursing mothers, nearby barking dogs, and a few small children actively about in the back of the church.

Their singing began to bring tears to my eyes as they expressed to the Lord their love for him. Then it hit me,

The Vigil

someday every Christian from every people group, every nation, continent, and tiny village like More Tomorrow will gather before the King of Kings, and with one voice somehow will present indescribable beauty in worship to the Lord of Glory. Only with the Lord in heaven will this level of worship be possible.

In order to really understand the Lord we worship and serve requires the multi-dimensional properties of heaven to adequately acknowledge God and give him deserving honor. How on earth with our finite ability could we ever truly and effectively present enough words, prayers, music, or any art form to really honor him?

Another of David's offerings as he attempts to praise God and present His character and qualities is this:

"Praise the Lord, O my soul. O Lord my God, you are very great; you are clothed with splendor and majesty. He wraps Himself in light as with a garment;

He stretches out the heavens like a tent and lays the beams of his upper chambers on their waters.

He makes the clouds His chariot and rides on the wings of the wind.

The Vigil

He makes winds His messengers, flames of fire His servants.[56]
"

I believe in the infallibility of Scripture, and I mean no disrespect or dishonor in any way, but I think even David's abilities as a lyricist and composer of songs fails to provide adequate mental visuals to present God in all his wonder. How do you wrap your mind around someone who makes the clouds his chariot and walks on the wings of the wind? Let's be honest, you can't.

And so, the prayer model of Jesus and the outline he gave us for life ends with the offering of acknowledgement and declaration to God as the only being worthy to receive worship. He is all-inclusive, self-sustaining, and inexhaustible. He is God, and to him be the glory forever and ever, holy is his name.

"May You be praised, Lord God of our father Israel, from eternity to eternity. Yours, Lord, is the greatness and the power and the glory and the splendor and the majesty, for everything in the heavens and on earth belongs to You. Yours, Lord, is the kingdom, and You are exalted as head over all. Riches and honor come from You, and You are the ruler of everything. In Your

hand are power and might, and it is in Your hand to make great and to give strength to all. Now therefore, our God, we give You thanks and praise Your glorious name."[57]

For Yours is the Kingdom and the power
and the glory forever. Amen.

Epilogue: A Life of Excellence

God, the blessed and only Ruler, the King of kings and Lord of Lords, who alone is immortal and who lives in unapproachable light, whom no one has seen or can see. To him be honor and might forever. Amen.[58]

Life can only be experienced as intended when lived in its singularly designed context. Otherwise, we are attempting to put the preverbal square peg in the round hole.

God has designed for each individual within humanity a life defined and planned by him, and even then only with his help can we accurately execute it. Our part is to simply say, "Yes!" to him.

Try as we may to experience real life on our own we will always fail, even though we can deceive ourselves into sometimes thinking we have succeeded. We will never come close to drafting a plan for ourselves that equals God's, never!

He is life's master craftsman and apart from him all attempts at gratification and fulfillment are temporary. It is after all as the oft-quoted phrase says "all about God!"

He made us for the purpose of living a life of worship in

honor and exalting him. Humanity is frail and fragile, yet we are invited to become of incalculable importance as we surrender before God. We become his possession, his friend, one of his very children.

One quiet Sunday evening I was at my desk enjoying some writing time while my wife was in the next room addressing invitations for an upcoming birthday party, and our youngest son was on the sofa reading a book. It was very peaceful until the uninvited sound of sirens began to intrude in the distance, breaking the silence.

Even though they were still a good distance away, they were approaching fast and becoming louder. The wind was brisk, and we had been experiencing a very dry season, so I thought it might be the local volunteer fire department en route to extinguish a brushfire somewhere nearby since there had already been a couple fires breakout in recent days.

I noticed the sirens stopped as I continued writing, but then through the window I saw a flashing blue light as it pierced the darkness across the field in our small valley. It was an emergency vehicle carefully making its way along our rough narrow country road.

We would later discover it was a deputy sheriff's car, and

the first of four emergency vehicles to follow down the lane past our home to our neighbor's house. A minute or so after the first car an ambulance also cautiously maneuvered the lane.

Concern quickly grew in the three of us for our elderly neighbor and longtime friend, Sue Haggard, who had lived in the two-story house nestled in the trees at the end of the dirt and gravel lane for about thirty years.

I called her home phone as soon as I saw the first car, but there was no response, so when we saw the ambulance my son and I quickly jumped in the car and drove to Sue's house.

Within a hundred yards of reaching her home, we could see several cars, some with emergency lights still flashing. We parked about fifty yards away from her home in case the ambulance needed to get out quickly and we walked through the darkness toward the light beside her backdoor.

There was a season in our lives years ago when we would often enter our neighbor's home through the backdoor entrance like family might. Many evenings of laughter, home cooked meals, fellowship, and prayer had occurred in the rooms just beyond that back porch door we were now approaching.

By this time both my son and I suspected the news would probably not be good, but neither of us said anything to the

The Vigil

other.

An officer walked out just about the time we arrived. We approached and told him we were friends and neighbors and asked if he could tell us what had occurred. He simply replied that an elderly woman had died. My son and I stood outside for a while in silence, knowing a chapter in life had firmly closed.

Though we hadn't seen much of our neighbor in recent years, except the occasional greeting while passing each other along the bumpy drive, there was a time when we would visit with Sue and her husband Gene several times a week in their home. She and her husband had great impact on our lives after we first moved to Arkansas.

There were few promises that accompanied the invitation to move to Arkansas to take our first ministry position. We knew only a few people in the area, had very little beyond a desire to serve God, but this couple took my wife and I under their wings for quite some time.

The Haggard's encouraged us, took us out for numerous meals, invited us over for holidays when we couldn't afford to go home to Louisville or didn't have a car we thought would make the trip.

Once when we had to move from a small upstairs apartment

and were looking for a place to live they fixed up a little house they owned next to their home and invited us to call that our home for a while.

They were kind, had a simple love and devotion to Christ, one another, and were like a second set of parents to us as well as many other singles and young married couples.

I was sad when her husband Gene had died several years earlier, and now my son and I were standing outside her home in the darkness leaning on an emergency vehicle each wishing we had taken time to see her once more.

A week earlier I had thought about driving down for a quick visit, but didn't. When my grandson was born I thought several times about taking him to see her so she could meet the little guy, but again the thought was, "I'll do it the next time he's here for a visit."

Now it will never be possible. My neighbor lived a fruitful and long life, but I still think about how it would have been good to talk to her one more time.

A few weeks before this situation occurred I shared in a memorial service for a much younger woman, another friend, but one who led a very rough life most of her years.

Lisa began using opiates in her late teens and remained

The Vigil

addicted to them most of her life. I met her years later after she had moved from California to Arkansas and opened a little café not far from my office.

We became friends and eventually she started coming to our church. Lisa visited and watched us for almost a year because she didn't really trust people who said they were Christians. Finally she decided there was something she saw in most of the folks in the church that she desired to have in her own life and she surrendered her life to Jesus.

I will never forget the huge smile on Lisa's face the day I raised her from the water during her baptism. She was very excited to have a new chance at life and to learn more of Christ.

Life was not easy for Lisa, but her friends said her time spent in fellowship with other Christians were the years she really loved. A few years passed and she returned to California, and one day I received a call that she had died, her liver had failed from the long-term effects of drug abuse and her system just shut down.

In spite of the sadness caused by the loss of a friend, I was reminded that she was finally free. Free of the consequences of years of drugs and free to experience eternal life with Jesus, the life after physical death.

Stories and memorials of the final chapters of people's lives are accumulating as my years in ministry increase.

Each time one takes place I am reminded of life's fragility and brevity. Even what we call *a good, long life*, is still a fleeting moment at best, and once it is over, we are not granted a do over to adjust things we would do differently in hindsight.

We all hope for long, healthy lives, but the truth is we have no idea of the number of our days, only that the Bible tells us to be very wise concerning how we live them, because once they pass they cannot be retrieved.

There are a lot of books and magazines lining store shelves concerning how to live the best life, and I am grateful for those that point us to Jesus and the example he lived.

His was a life given to the will of his Father in heaven. His was a pattern of prayer, devotion, and grace as he dispensed truth that would lead to life beyond the ephemeral. His was a life of spiritual vigilance, of giving to others while motivated by love. Shouldn't ours be also?

The word vigil is not one often heard in conversations at the local corner café over lattes and mocha's.

When it is used, more than not it brings to mind the painting from antiquity of a small candle lit room on a cold winter's eve, an elderly gentleman in his 80's, hands folded, head bowed as he kneels praying at a simple wooden bench, a large worn leather bound Bible opened before him, with a tiny four-pane window covered with frost just above his head on the wall.

Perhaps the word vigil reminds us of people clustered together in one location praying and awaiting news of possible survivor's in a collapsed coal mine, a small fishing boat lost at sea or a downed plane in the snow covered Rocky Mountain wilderness.

I wonder though when we think of a vigil as a time set aside to focus in depth on drawing near to God, and when we consider the brevity of this life on earth in the context of eternity, would we be amiss to view and approach the whole of Christian life as one spent in vigil?

We have seventy or so years that whip past like fallen leaves driven across the landscape before a strong spring thunder storm, and yet so much of it is squandered on a quest to secure better creature comforts for ourselves in this life. Could it be the normal Christian life was intended to be one spent in spiritual vigilance?

I'm not suggesting a life of poverty, legalism, or living all of life alone in the desert. Jesus told us to love God with all of our heart, soul, mind, and strength, to love our neighbor as we love ourselves and to go throughout the world and make Christ followers.

Is it possible we are missing something? Is it possible we have drifted from the plumb line, the archetype? It seems the Bible tells us that the Kingdom of God is about relationship:

- Relationship with God
- Relationship with one another
- Leading others into this relationship

We are to love and worship God, see his kingdom come and will done, not worry about provision because he resources what he wills, and trust him to lead and protect us as we serve Him . As the Scripture tells us, "The world and its desires pass away, but the man who does the will of God lives forever."[59]

We have created nothing, we own nothing, and all we have is loaned to us to properly steward as we follow the course God directs.

Some amass huge stockpiles of wealth, only to surrender it upon transitioning from this earth to heaven or hell accordingly as to the belief system of choice.

Over the weekend when writing this chapter a devastating

storm hit a town not far from us and in minutes turned a large percentage of it into a scrap heap. Story after story was heard of people who had lost everything, many who had spent their lives acquiring and building what they had, only to surrender it to an indifferent wind.

We never know when our lives may change in an instant. That is why we are encouraged by Jesus to not focus on the things of this world, but to seek first the Kingdom of God and his righteousness.

Since the whole earth is filled with his glory, and all things are created by him and for him. Since our time on this earth is like a fleeting moment and our intended design by God is live for his glory, his pleasure, why would we treasure anything else?

The whole earth, all it contains, all the universes beyond, from the smallest to the largest created thing, it is all his, it all exists for his glory! So could I challenge you to join with me in this vigil?

Would you stand with the millions of Christians throughout the ages as together we live the words we pray.

Our Father in heaven, Your name be honored as holy.

Your kingdom come.

Your will be done on earth as it is in heaven.

Give us today our daily bread. And forgive us our debts,

as we also have forgiven our debtors.

And do not bring us into temptation,

but deliver us from the evil one.

For Yours is the kingdom and the power

and the glory forever. Amen.[60]

The Village2Village Story

Village2Village was birthed in February 2010 while I was spending a few days alone in a small 10X14 foot cabin about two hundred yards from the Belize River in the tiny community of Banana Bank. It was not my first mission trip or visit to another country because I have made several such trips over the years, but for some reason this one had an unusual effect on me.

One rainy morning I was sitting at small table writing some thoughts in a notebook, when the sound of the drops hitting the tin metal roof began to subside. As it did I put my pen down, looked up through the small window and watched a colorful tropical bird land on the branches of a nearby tree. In the distance was the voice of a male Howler monkey letting others know that he was the territorial authority and willing to meet challengers if necessary.

While gazing through the window I began to think of the people I had seen the couple of days before as I visited several small villages. I remembered the smiles of small children tossing coconuts, playing soccer with a makeshift ball of some kind, huts with dirt floors, bamboo poles for walls, and palm leaf roofs. Metal grates placed over stones for open fire cooking inside the huts. People bathing, playing, and cleaning clothes in streams and rivers, then hauling water in containers back along dusty roads and paths, to their dwellings. The names of More Tomorrow, San Pablo, Dump, Valley of Peace, or even Belmopan the country's capitol city were only places I had heard one missionary speak of. Now those villages had faces and situations attached to them.

The Vigil

I felt I wanted and needed to attempt to do more than just help support the few missionaries our church was assisting. We had stretched our churches mission budget about as much as we could and yet there were so many worthy people I knew that needed and could use help. That is when in my mind the "What Ifs'" began to materialize and make their presence known.

"What if I could do and be more involved somehow?"

"What if I could use what influence I might have to help raise the awareness, and support of missionaries I know and I am getting to know?"

"What if I could begin to mobilize friends and acquaintances not currently connected or involved in missions into helping others in the mission field and get them interested and involved also?"

"What if we could begin to make products and the profits could go to assist those working to help others and the people and projects they are engaged in?"

"What if a growing community of friends developed focused on helping others?"

I realize there are many organizations doing the same or similar thing as Village2Village, but there is also plenty of need in our world. The need is actually so overwhelming; many do not know where to begin or which group to support. Village2Village is merely building a community of people linked together to do our part with the people we are already in relationship with and people we are building relationship with.

As of the writing of these pages, an example of what V2V is currently involved in would be a school in Kampala, Uganda we are trying to build. We are assisting an indigenous pastor there who has become a friend with his vision of serving the people in the region in which he lives. The school began with a few children but has quickly grown to over 80 young students. These students are being given an opportunity to better help themselves and their futures though this Christian based school operated by dedicated people sacrificing to serve their community.

The meal the students receive each day is often their best, which typically made up of a bowl of rice and beans, and chicken when possible. We are hoping to help complete this school which when finished will accommodate additional students and house six teachers plus provide ongoing funding for this school into the future.

V2V is also involved with supporting multiple missionaries and their multifaceted ministries in Belize and Thailand.

Please visit www.village2village.co for more information.

You can check out Craig's recent book and music project, *"Ancient Path"* along with his other projects by visiting
www.craigsmithmusic.co
or
www.amazon.com

Don't forgot to check out
"The Vigil" Book of Prayer
and *"The Vigil"* CD or download
while you are there!

References

[1] John R. W. Stott, *The Message of the Sermon On The Mount* (Downers Grove: Inter-Varsity Press,1978), p. 147, 148.

[2] Matthew Henry's Commentary on the New Testament

[3] John Piper, *A Hunger for God* (Wheaton: Crossway Books, 1997), p.21.

[4] Sinclair B Ferguson, *The Sermon On The Mount* (Carlisle: The Banner Of Truth Trust, 1987), p. 120.

[5] Matthew 6:9-13 HCSB

[6] Craig Smith

[7] Proverbs 13:20 NIV

[8] James G. S.S. Thomson, *The Praying Christ* (Grand Rapids: Eerdmans Publishing Co., 1959), p. 86

[9] 1 Peter 2:9 NIV

[10] Adam Clark,John M'clintock and James Strong, eds., *Clclopedia of Biblical, Theological, and Ecclesiastical Literature,* vol. 3 (New York: Harper and Brothers, 1894), pp. 903-904. From Dallas Willard, *The Divine Conspiracy* (San Francisco: Harper/Collins, 1998), p. 65, 66.

[11] Robert Jamieson, A.R. Fausset, and David Brown, *A Commentary Critical, Experimental, and Practical on the Old and New Testaments* (Originally published by S.S. SCRANTON, HARTFORD, 1877. Reprinted Grand Rapids: Eerdmans Publishing Co., 1993)

[12] Arthur W. Pink, *An Exposition of the Sermon on the Mount,* (Grand Rapids, Mich: Baker Book House, 1950), p162.

[13] Psalms 66:4 NIV

[14] Hebrews 2:20 NIV

[15] Psalms 46:10 NLT

[16] Psalms 115:1 NIV

[17] Isaiah 26:8,9 NIV

[18] Psalms 8:9 NKJV

[19] Exodus 3:13,14 NIV

[20] Colossians 3:18 NLT

[21] Ephesians 5:20 Ibid

[22] Psalms 113: 1,2 NLT

[23] Sinclair B. Ferguson, *The Sermon on the Mount,*(Carlisle: The Banner of Truth Trust, 1984), p. 123.

[24] James G. S.S. Thomson, *The Praying Christ* (Grand Rapids: Eerdmans Publishing Co., 1959), p.91,92

[25] Psalms 145:10-13 NIV

[26] (from Sermons of John Wesley, PC Study Bible formatted electronic database Copyright © 2003, 2006

[27] Matthew 26:39 HCSB

The Vigil

[28] John 1:3, 4 HCSB

[29] John 10:10 IBID

[30] Psalms 143:10 HCSB

[31] N.T. Wright, The Lord and His Prayer, William B. Eerdmans Publishing co: Grand Rapids, MI. (1996), p36.

[32] Barnes Notes, Electronic database copyright 1997, Biblesoft Inc.

[33] Proverbs 3:27,28 HCSB

[34] Craig Smith

[35] Psalms 51:7 NLT

[36] Luke 18:9-14 HCSB

[37] Sinclair B Ferguson, The Sermon on the Mount, The Banner of truth Trust, Carlisle: 1987.

[38] Luke 23:31 – 35 NIV

[39] Acts 7:59, 60 HCSB

[40] N. T. Wright, The Lord and His prayer, William B. Eerdmans Publishing co: Grand Rapids, MI.,(1996), p54.

[41] Matthew 6:14, 15 HCSB

[42] Mark 11:14 HCSB

[43] N. T. Wright, The Lord and His Prayer, William B. Eerdmans Publishing co: Grand Rapids, MI.,(1996), pages 67,68.

[44] James 1:13 NLT

[45] Mark 14:35, 36 NLT

[46] All Psalms references in this list from the NIV

[47] John R. W. Stott, The message of the Sermon on the Mount, Inter-Varsity Press: Leicester, England,(1978), p150

[48] Psalms 23:4 NIV

[49] Isaiah 41:10 NLT

[50] Mark 6:50 HCSB

[51] Psalms 56: 3,4 HCSB

[52] John 17:15-16 NIV

[53] Psalms 27:1 NIV

[54] Revelation 4:11 NIV

[55] Psalms 106:1, 2 HCSB

[56] Psalms 104:1-5 HCSB

[57] 1 Chronicles 29:10-13 HCSB

[58] 1 Timothy 6:15,16 NIV

[59] 1 John 2:17 NIV

[60] Matthew 6:9-13 HCSB

Made in the USA
Charleston, SC
08 March 2013